Betamarine Beta 10, BZ482, Beta 16 (BZ602), BD722 & Beta 25 (BD902)

Maintenance Manual

Betamarine Beta 10, BZ482, Beta 16 (BZ602), BD722 & Beta 25 (BD902)

Maintenance Manual

ISBN/EAN: 9783954275014
Erscheinungsjahr: 2012
Erscheinungsort: Bremen, Deutschland

© *maritimepress in Europäischer Hochschulverlag GmbH & Co. KG, Fahrenheitstr. 1, 28359 Bremen. Alle Rechte beim Verlag und bei den jeweiligen Lizenzgebern.*

www.maritimepress.de | office@maritimepress.de

Bei diesem Titel handelt es sich um den Nachdruck eines historischen, lange vergriffenen Buches. Da elektronische Druckvorlagen für diese Titel nicht existieren, musste auf alte Vorlagen zurückgegriffen werden. Hieraus zwangsläufig resultierende Qualitätsverluste bitten wir zu entschuldigen.

Betamarine Beta 10, BZ482, Beta 16 (BZ602), BD722 & Beta 25 (BD902)

Maintenance Manual

Contents

INTRODUCTION   2
Engine Identification   2
Initial Receipt of the engine   2
Engine Storage   2

SAFETY PRECAUTIONS   3

TECHNICAL SPECIFICATIONS   4

SECTION 1: GUIDELINES FOR OPERATION OF ENGINE
Important checks prior to initial use   5
Initial Start-up and Bleeding The Fuel System   5
Starting/Stopping   6

SECTION 2: MAINTENANCE AND SERVICE GUIDELINES
Maintenance Schedule: 7
Lubrication – Checking and changing oil   8
Fuel System - Pumps, Filter, fuel/water separator   9
Cooling - Fresh water system, Keel Cooling, Heat Exchanger   10
Sea Water Pump, Heat Exchanger   12
Belt Tensioning   13
Air Filter   13
Electrical   14
Laying up - Winterising   14
Troubleshooting   15
Torque Settings   26

SECTION 3: INSTALLATION GUIDELINES
Engine Mounting   27
Alignment - Drives, Flanges, Flexible Drives   27
Exhausts & Bends   28
Mounting Exhausts   28
Fuel Supply   29
Cooling   30
Calorifier System   31
Electrical installations   32
Appendices –wiring diagrams and general arrangements   32
Component identification at rear of manual.   63
Maintenance Record   65

OPERATION AND MAINTENANCE MANUAL FOR THE FOLLOWING
BETA MARINE ENGINES BASED ON KUBOTA MINI SERIES

Beta 10, BZ482, Beta 16 (BZ602), BD722 & Beta 25 (BD902)

This manual has been compiled to provide the user with important information and recommendations to ensure a trouble free and economical operation of the engine.

For further advice or technical assistance, application should be made to BETA MARINE LIMITED or its distributors.

All information and recommendations given in this publication are based on the latest information available at the time of publication, and are subject to alteration at any time. The information given is subject to the company's current conditions of Tender and Sale, is for the assistance of users, and is based upon results obtained from tests carried out at the place of manufacture and in vessels used for development purposes. We do not guarantee the same results will be obtained elsewhere under different conditions.

ENGINE IDENTIFICATION

NOTE: In all communications with the distributor or Beta Marine, **the engine number, type, and W.O.C. number must be quoted.**

BETA 10, BZ482, BETA 16, BD722 & BETA 25

The engine serial number is stamped above the fuel lift pump on the starboard side of the engine, and is shown on the rocker cover label.

INITIAL RECEIPT OF THE ENGINE

A full inspection of the engine must be made _**immediately on delivery**_ to confirm that there is no damage. If there is any damage then write this clearly on the delivery note and inform your dealer or Beta Marine within 24 hours.

ENGINE STORAGE

The engine must be stored in a dry, frost free area and this is best done in its packing case. If storage is to be more than six months then the engine must be inhibited (contact your dealer or Beta Marine). Failure to inhibit the engine may result in the formation of rust in the injection system and the engine bores, this could invalidate the warranty.

SAFETY PRECAUTIONS!

A Keep the engine, gearbox and surrounding area clean, including the area immediately below the engine

B DRIVES - Power Take Off Areas

i) Gearbox Output Flange

The purpose of a marine diesel propulsion engine is to provide motive power to propel a vessel. Accordingly the gearbox output shaft rotates at between 300 and 2400 rev/min. This flange is designed to be coupled to a propeller shaft by the installer and steps must be taken to ensure adequate guarding.

ii) Forward End Drive

Engines are supplied with unguarded vee belt drives to power the fresh water pump and battery charging alternator. The installer must ensure that it is not possible for injury to occur by allowing accessibility to this area of the engine. The three pulleys run at high speed and can cause injury if personnel or clothing come in contact with the belts or pulleys, when the engine is running.

iii) Power Take Off Shaft (Engine Mounted Option)

Shaft extensions are available as an option and rotate at between 850 and 3600 rev/min. If contact is made with this shaft when the engine is running, injury can occur.

C EXHAUST OUTLET

Diesel marine propulsion engines emit exhaust gases at very high temperatures - around 400-500°C. Engines are supplied with either wet exhaust outlet (water injection bend) or dry outlet (dry exhaust stub) - see option list. At the outlet next to the heat exchanger/header tank, the exhaust outlet can become very hot and if touched, can injure. This must be lagged or avoided by ensuring adequate guarding. It is the responsibility of the installer to lag the exhaust system if a dry system is used. Exhaust gases are harmful if ingested, the installer must therefore ensure that exhaust lines are lead overboard and that leakage in the vessel does not occur.

D FUEL

i) Fuel Lines

Diesel engines are equipped with high pressure fuel injection pumps, if leakages occur, or if pipes fracture, fuel at a high pressure can harm personnel. Skin must be thoroughly cleaned in the event of contact with diesel fuel.

ii) Fuel Supply Connections

Engines are supplied with 8 mm compression fittings. The installer must ensure that when connections are made, they are clean and free of leaks.

E OIL

The Beta propulsion is supplied with 2 dipsticks, one for the engine and one for the gearbox. Ensure dipsticks are returned and secure after checking, if not oil leaks can cause infection when touched. All oil must be removed from the skin to prevent infection.

F SCALDING

An engine running under load will have a closed circuit fresh water temperature of 85° to 95°C. The pressure cap on the top of the heat exchanger must not be removed when the engine is running. It can only be removed when the engine is stopped and has cooled down.

G TRANSPORTATION/LIFTING

Engines are supplied on transportable pallets. Lifting eyes on engines are used for lifting engine and gearbox assembly only, not the pallet and associated kit.

GENERAL DECLARATION

This machinery is not intended to be put into
service until it has been incorporated into or with other machinery. It is the responsibility of the purchaser/installer/owner, to ensure that the machinery is properly guarded and that all necessary health and safety requirements, in accordance with the laws of the relevant country, are met before it is put into service.

Signed:

J A Growcoot, C.E.O,
Beta Marine Limited

NOTE: Recreational Craft

Where applicable, the purchaser/installer/owner and operator must be responsible for making sure that the Recreational Craft Directive 94/25/EC is complied with.

TECHNICAL SPECIFICATIONS

MINI SERIES – STANDARD ENGINES

	BETA 10	BZ482	Beta 16	BD722	Beta 25
Cylinder	2	2	2	3	3
Bore (mm)	67	67	72	67	72
Stroke (mm)	68	68	73.6	68	73.6
Displacement (cc)	479	479	599	719	898
Combustion	3 Vortex E-TVCS				
Cooling	Water				
Starter voltage (V)	12				
Starter output (kW)	0.8				
Starter alternator output (Amps)	40 (standard)				
Glow plug resistance (each)	1Ω				
Engine speed (RPM)	3,000		3,600		
Power output to ISO3046 (BHP)	10.0	13.3	16.7	20.0	24.8
Declared power ISO8665 (kW)	7.4	8.7	11.0	13.1	16.3
Fuel timing BTDC	21°				
Capacity of standard sump approx (litres)	2.0 - 2.5		2.4 - 2.9	3.1 - 3.8	3.7 – 4.5
Capacity of shallow sump approx (litres)	2.2		2.6	3.4	3.8
Nett dry weight with gearbox (kg)	87.2		94.1	101.7	110.6
Fuel	Diesel oil class A1 / A2				
Coolant	33%-50% maximum antifreeze / water				
Coolant capacity approx (H/E litres)	2.25			3.00	3.25
Min. recommended battery capacity	12V, 40Ah			12V, 75Ah	

Maximum Angle of Installation: Trim 15°, Roll 30° (intermittent)
Rotation: ANTI CLOCK ON FLYWHEEL, CLOCKWISE ON OUTPUT GEARBOX FLANGE FOR USE **WITH RIGHT HAND PROP IN AHEAD**
Diesel fuel must conform to BS2869-1970 class A1 or A2. The fuel must be a distillate, and not a residual oil or blend.
Lubricant: Engine - Engine oil must meet MIL-L-2104C (see section 2 for details)
  Gearbox - see operator's manual for the gearbox oil type and capacity
  Oil pressure – minimum (tickover) 0.5 bar
Power outputs: These comply with BS EN ISO 8665:1996 crankshaft power
Note: Declared Powers to ISO8665:1995
1. **The declared powers are at the same engine speed as the ISO 3046 figures. This speed is the speed related to the outputs / powers shown.**
2. Declared powers are at the gearbox coupling (coupling to the propeller shaft) as per clause 3.2.1 with standard specifications as per our current price lists. Additional accessories or alternative gearboxes may affect the declared powers.
3. Operation at parameters outside the test parameters may affect the outputs / powers which in any case are subject to the ISO tolerance bands.

SECTION 1

GUIDELINES FOR OPERATION OF ENGINE

IMPORTANT CHECKS PRIOR TO INITIAL USE

1. Generally, a new engine has the oil and anti-freeze removed after the works test. Fill the engine with the correct oil and anti-freeze (see sections on ENGINE OIL and COOLING). Check gearbox oil level - see separate operator's hand book.

2. Ensure the engine is free to turn without obstructions.

3. Ensure battery is fully charged and connected (the isolator is in the 'ON' position).

4. Ensure Morse speed and gearbox cables are fitted correctly and that cable travel lengths are correct. Gear selection lever –all mechanical gearboxes: care must be taken to ensure that the remote control cable is adjusted so that the selector lever on the gearbox moves FULL travel and brought "hard up" against its end stop in both directions. Failure to achieve the correct adjustment will reduce efficiency of the clutch and may cause slippage at low revs. Warranty will not be accepted on gearboxes returned in the warranty period for failure due to incorrect adjustment.

5. Ensure engine **is out of gear** with 1/3 throttle - see single lever control instruction manual.

6. Open the fuel stopcock and bleed the fuel water separator of air as shown in manufacturers literature.

7. Fuel should now be at the fuel lift pump, see diagram 1a.

8. Open the sea cock.

INITIAL STARTUP AND BLEEDING THE SYSTEM

(a) Open fuel bleed screw on injection pump by 1½ turns. See diagram 1a.

(b) Move hand priming lever on fuel lift pump up and down until fuel with no bubbles comes out of the bleed screw.

(c) Shut/tighten the bleed screw. Clean area thoroughly with tissue paper.

(d) Continue to hand prime for 30 seconds to push fuel through the fuel pump.

(e) Start engine (see normal starting).

Note the engine may have to be turned over with the starter for a few seconds before it fires. Do not run the starter for more than 20 seconds. If the engine has not started after 20 seconds then disengage the starter and continue to hand prime for a further 30 seconds, then repeat.

(f) If engine does not start after 3 attempts then allow 5 minutes for the starter to cool down before repeating (a) to (e).

Note: The starter windings can be burnt out with continuous cranking

CAUTION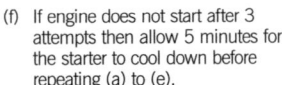

To avoid personal injury:

- Do not bleed a hot engine as this could cause fuel to spill onto a hot exhaust manifold creating a danger of fire.
- Do not mix gasoline or alcohol with diesel fuel. This mixture can cause an explosion.
- Do not get diesel on the flexible mounts – they will deteriorate rapidly if soaked in diesel.
- All fuel must be removed from skin to prevent infection.

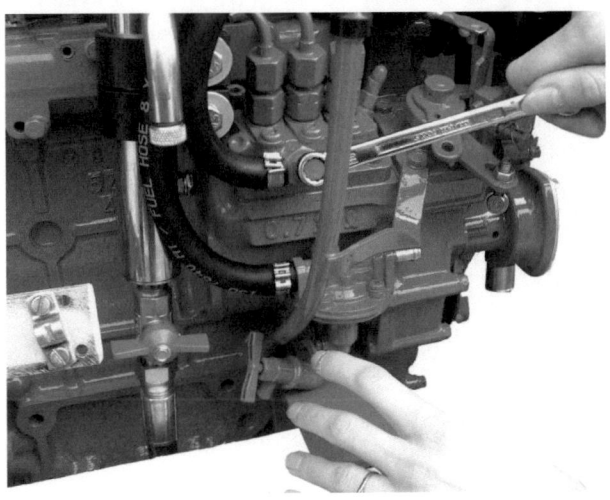

Diagram 1a

NORMAL STARTING (ALL BETA PANELS WITH SILVER KEYSWITCH)

With the engine out of gear, set speed control lever to 1/3 throttle. Turn key anti-clockwise to HEAT* (A) position and hold for ten seconds, turn key clockwise to RUN (C) position. At this stage the instrument panel should illuminate, an alarm buzzer will sound and two (or three*) red warning lights will illuminate:

STARTER BATTERY CHARGE

DOMESTIC BATTERY CHARGE* (D in battery symbol - AB & C PANELS ONLY)

*(**Note**: this will only illuminate if 2nd alternator is fitted)

OIL PRESSURE and green POWER ON / RUN LIGHT (this will stay on)

Turn to START (D) position and engine will motor, hold in position until engine fires (see initial start-up section for maximum time starter can be used).

Release key (when engine has started) to RUN position. Ensure alarm buzzer is not sounding and that warning lights are extinguished. If one or both of the alternator warning lights are still on, then increase engine speed to excite the alternator - then return to idle. The battery charge lights should then go out. The run light will remain on (green LED).

Note: for panels without keyswitches see seperate instruction sheet (page 24).

STOPPING

Every propulsion engine is fitted with a stop solenoid which is energised to stop. To stop engine simply press stop push button, hold in until engine stops, then turn key from 'RUN' to 'OFF' position.

When leaving the boat for an extended period,
- Turn off sea-cock (heat exchanger cooled engines).
- Turn off battery isolator.

Do not turn the key to the off position when the engine is running. This will not allow the alternator to charge.

*WARNING /

Do not leave the key in 'HEAT' position for more than 15 seconds - this will damage the heater plugs and eventually lead to poor starting.

Do not depress stop button for more than 10 seconds as this will lead to overheating and failure of the solenoid.

NOTES FOR ALL PANEL TYPES:

Do not depress the stop button for more than ten seconds as this will lead to overheating and failure of the solenoid.

The Mini range of engines are equipped with a mechanical stop lever in the event of electrical system failure. This lever is located on the starboard side of the engine above the speed control lever. See illustration below:

SECTION 2

MAINTENANCE SCHEDULE

DAILY OR EVERY 8 HOURS RUNNING

- Check engine oil level.
- Check gearbox oil level.
- Check coolant level.
- Check battery fluid.
- Check drive belt tension
- Ensure raw water inlet strainer is clear.
- Check stern gland lubrication.
- Drain off any water in fuel water separator.

AFTER THE FIRST 25 HOURS RUNNING

- Change gearbox lubricant (See separate gearbox manual).
- Check that all external nuts, bolts and fastenings are tight. See table for torque values. Special attention should be paid to the flexible mount lock nuts, these should be checked for tightness, starting with lower nut first in each case. If the lower nuts are found to be very loose, then the alignment of the shaft to the gearbox half coupling should be re-checked. Poor alignment due to loose flexible mount nuts will cause excessive vibration and knocking.
- Check the belt tension on any second alternators fitted and adjust –see page 11
- Check ball joint nyloc nuts for tightness on both gearbox and speed control levers. Grease both fittings all over.

AFTER FIRST 50 HOURS

- Change engine lubricating oil.
- Change oil filter.
- Check for leaks on header tank tubestack. Tighten end cap bolt if required.
- Drain off any water in fuel/water separator.

EVERY 150 HOURS

- If shallow sump (option) is fitted, change engine lubricating oil and filter.

EVERY YEAR -OR EVERY 250 HOURS IF SOONER

- Change engine lubricating oil (standard sump)
- Change lubricating oil filter
- Check air cleaner element
- Check sea water pump impeller and change if worn.
- Check wasting anode condition, replace when necessary. In some environments this may be 6 montly or less.
- Remove heat exchanger tube stack, by undoing the bolt each end of the tube stack. Remove end cover, pull out tube stack and clean. Replace rubber 'O' rings and re-assemble. Immediately engine is started check for leaks.
- Spray the key switch with WD40 or equivalent to lubricate the barrel.
- Check that all external nuts, bolts and fastenings are tight. See table for torque values.
- Check ball joint nyloc nuts for tightness on both gearbox and speed control levers. Grease both fittings all over.

EVERY 750 HOURS

- As every 250 hours plus the following:-
- Change air cleaner element.
- Change fuel filter.
- Change antifreeze.
- Change gearbox oil.
- Check electrical equipment, condition of hoses and belts, replace as necessary.

LUBRICATION

Engine oil: Engine oil should be MIL-L-2104C or have properties of API classification CC/CD/CE grades. The following table gives grades of oil required for various ambient temperatures.

Note: A good quality 15W/40 mineral or multigrade oil as used in most diesel car engines will meet these requirements. Do not use 'Turbo Diesel Oil' or additives.

1. To check the oil level, draw out the dipstick, wipe it clean, re-insert it, and draw it out again. Check to see that the oil level lies between the two notches.
2. If the level is too low, add new oil to the specified level - Do not overfill.

IMPORTANT ⚠

When using an oil of different make or viscosity from the previous one, drain old oil. Never mix two different types of oil. Engine oil should be changed after first 50 hours running time and then every year or every 250 hours if sooner. Oil filter is a cartridge type mounted on the port side of the engine.

CHECKING ENGINE OIL LEVEL

For quantities of oil required see section marked 'Technical Specification', Page 4

When checking the engine oil level, do so before starting, or more than five minutes after stopping.

AMBIENT TEMP	SINGLE GRADE	MULTI GRADE
-30°C TO 0°C	SAE 10W S	AE 10W/30
-15°C TO +15°C	SAE 20W	SAE 15W/40
0°C TO +30°C	SAE 30	SAE 15W/40
25°C AND ABOVE	SAE 30	SAE 15W/40

CHANGING ENGINE OIL

(1) Run the engine for 10 minutes to warm up the oil.

(2) Your engine is provided with a sump drain pump (option on Beta Ten, see note below). Unscrew the end cap on the end of the pump (if fitted), turn the tap to 'on'. Use the hand pump as shown to pump out the oil into a bucket. Turn the tap to off position and replace end cap. See diagram 2c.

(3) Unscrew the oil filter and replace with a new one. See diagram 2d.

Note: It is best to have a plastic bag wrapped round the filter to catch any oil left in the system. (Always keep your bilges clean!) Before screwing in the new filter spread a thin film of oil round the rubber gasket to ensure a good seal and screw in – hand tight.

Note: On the Beta Ten not fitted with a sump drain pump the engine oil must be drained off by unscrewing the sump drain plug (see diagram 100-00030 at rear of book). This is best done with the oil filler cap removed. Replace the plug and tighten firmly.

(4) Fill the engine with new oil as described above.

Oil goes in here

Fig. 2a

Fig. 2b. Dip stick

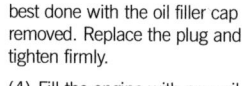

Sump pump

End Cap   Tap

Fig. 2c

Fig. 2d

Oil filter

CHECKING GEARBOX OIL LEVEL

(1) The gearbox is fitted with a dipstick and oil filler plug, see fig 2e.

(2) Each engine is supplied with a gearbox operators manual which specifies the type of lubricating oil to be used, the capacity and frequency of changing of the oil.

(3) New engines are normally supplied with the gearbox topped up with lubricant but Check the level before starting the engine for the first time.

(4) The oil can be changed via the drain plug at the bottom of the box or sucked out with a hand pump via the filler plug.

(5) A guide to the type of oil to be used is as follows:

Gearbox	Lubricant	Capacity (approx)
TMC40	Use ATF Oil	0.2 litres
PRM 80/120	Use Engine Oil 15W40	0.6 / 0.8 litres
ZF5M / ZF10M	Use ATF Oil	0.3 / 0.35 litres
TTMC 35A-2	Use Engine Oil SAE 30 (HD)	0.65 litres

Note: ATF is Automatic Transmission Fluid

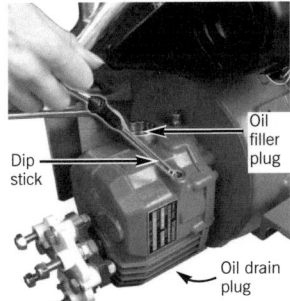

Fig 2e

FUEL SYSTEM (see page 29 for a typical installation)

IMPORTANT ⚠

- Always fit a fuel/water separator in the fuel supply system. **Water in the fuel can seriously damage the injection system.**

- If a fuel supply shutoff valve is fitted do not use a taper tap, only use a ball valve tap. The ball valve type are more reliable and less likely to let air into the fuel system.

- Be sure to use a strainer when filling the fuel tank. Dirt or sand in the fuel may cause trouble in the fuel injection pump.

- Always use diesel fuel.

- **Do not use kerosene** which is very low in cetane rating, and adversely affects the engine.

- Be careful not to let the fuel tank become empty, or air can enter the fuel system, necessitating bleeding before next engine start.

- The fuel lift pump will only lift fuel through 0.25 metres. If this is insufficient then an electric fuel lift pump must be fitted.

FUEL FILTER REPLACEMENT

1. The fuel filter is a spin on type. Remove by turning anti-clockwise when viewed from below.

2. Replace the fuel filter cartridge every 750 hours. See fig. 2g.

3. Apply fuel oil thinly over the gasket and tighten into position - hand tight.

4. Bleed as detailed - see initial start up.

5. Check for leaks.

6. **Do not get fuel on the flexible mounts.**

Fig. 2g

COOLING

The Mini Series range of engines are normally fresh water cooled. This water circulates through the engine and on to a heat exchanger where it is cooled by sea water which is pumped through the cooling tubes. The sea water is then injected into the exhaust system (see diagram 'heat exchanger cooled' below).

KEEL COOLING is an option. In this system the freshwater is pumped through the engine and then through a cooler built into the side of the boat where it is cooled by heat transfer before returning to the engine.

The ideal keel cooling tank should have:

a. Baffle continuously welded to outer skin and close fitting on inner skin
b. Be thin in section to allow good mixing of the water over the cool outer surface.
c. Air bleed valves should be fitted on both ends. (See page 30).

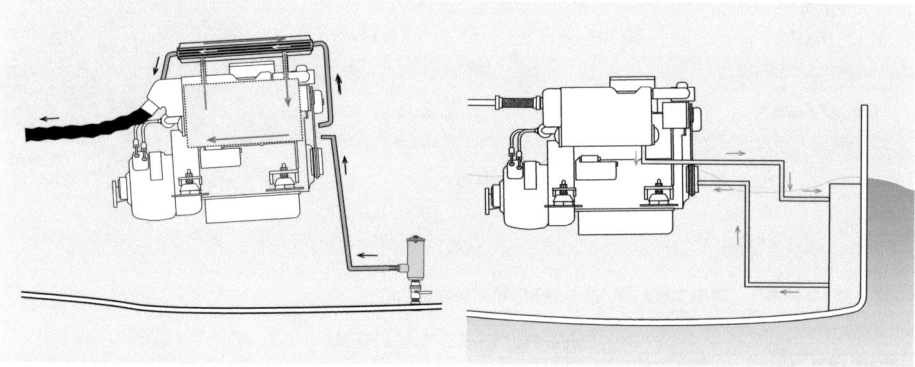

Heat Exchanger Cooled

Keel Cooled -Note efficient cooling tanks are side mounted, see page 31

FILLING THE FRESHWATER SYSTEM

New engines are supplied with the freshwater drained off. The following instructions must be followed to fill the system.

(a) Mix up in a clean bucket a 30 to 50% antifreeze to freshwater solution. For the volume required see technical specification page 4.

(b) Check that the drain tap or plug is turned off. (see fig 2l) (Note BZ482 and B10 engines with sump drain pump are fitted with a plug).

(c) Fill engine with freshwater/anti freeze solution through the top of the heat exchanger or header tank with the filler cap removed. (see fig 2m).

(d) Fill header tank to the top of the filler neck and replace cap. Press down firmly on filler cap and hand tighten in a clockwise direction.

Note: For keel cooled engines a much larger quantity of freshwater/anti-freeze solution is required depending on the size of the keel cooling tank – refer to the builder.

(e) Run the engine for 5 minutes on no load (out of gear) and check coolant level. Top up as necessary.

(f) Check system for leaks.

Note: For keel cooled engines it is very important to bleed all the air out of the system before the engine is run on load (check with builder's instructions).

(g) If a calorifier is fitted care must be taken to see that this is also full of coolant and all the air is expelled. (See calorifier fitting notes under Section 3).

(h) Run the engine on one third load for 15 minutes, preferably with the boat tied up. As the system warms up coolant may be expelled from the overflow pipe into the bilge. Stop the engine and allow the engine to cool down before removing the pressure cap and top up the coolant to 1" below the filler neck.

Fig. 2l

Fig. 2m

IMPORTANT ⚠

Removal of the pressure cap when the engine is hot can cause severe injury from scalding hot water under pressure. Always allow the engine to cool and then use a large cloth when turning the cap anti-clockwise to the stop. This allows the pressure to be released. Press firmly down on the cap and continue to turn anticlockwise to release the cap.

(i) Repeat (h) if coolant level is more than 1 inch below the base of the filler neck when the engine has cooled down.

(j) Run engine on 2/3 full load for 20 minutes, check for leaks and repeat (i).

(k) Anti-freeze solutions should be drained off every 2 years and replaced with a new solution.

Note: When draining fresh water system, ensure the engine has cooled sufficiently to prevent scalding from hot pressurised water. Prior to draining a cold engine, remove the filler cap from the header tank and then open the water drain tap. This allows the water to drain freely from the system.

YACHTS AND LAUNCHES WITH HEAT EXCHANGER COOLING

It is essential that a 33% to 50% anti-freeze/water mixture is used. This not only stops freezing up in winter, but it prevents overheating and corrosion.

The warranty is invalid unless the correct ratio is used.

CANAL BOATS WITH KEEL COOLER

A 33% anti-freeze to water mixture is recommended to give protection against very cold winter temperature of minus 15°C. This anti-freeze will also give the engine internal protection against corrosion. For keel cooled engines the total system capacity must be taken into consideration, ie engine volume plus skin tank/keel cooler volume.

Concentration of ethylene should not exceed 50%.

The anti-freeze in the fresh water system enables the boiling point of water to rise to 124°C with a 13 psi pressure cap fitted. The water temperature alarm switch will however be activated at 95° to 100°C. If no anti-freeze or a very weak solution is used, then the water temperature switch may not be activated before coolant is lost.

SEA WATER PUMP AND COOLING SYSTEM - (Heat exchanger-cooled engines)

CAUTION ⚠

Before working on the sea water system ensure **that the sea cock is in the off position**.

(1) It is very important that the correct sea water flow is maintained to cool the closed circuit system of the engine. The key component in this system is the sea water pump impeller. This should be checked every year by removing the circular plate (see fig. 2h)

(2) Withdraw the rubber impeller from its drive shaft as shown. See diagram 2i.

(3) Check impeller for cracks in the rubber, excessive wear or lost vanes. Replace with a new impeller as necessary.

Note: If any pieces of rubber impeller are missing then they must be found as they are most likely to be trapped in the entrance to the heat exchanger cooling stack. See 'Cleaning Tube Stack'.

Fig. 2h

Fig. 2i

CLEANING THE HEAT EXCHANGER TUBE STACK AND REPLACING WASTING ZINC ANODE

(1) The wasting zinc anode should be checked every six months and replaced every year or as necessary. The anode is attached to the bolt inserted in the aft end cap of the heat exchanger. See fig. 2j.

(2) Unscrew the bolt and replace the complete unit with a new one.

(3) Check for leaks.

(4) It is possible for fine sea weed and other debris to get past the inlet filter and into the tube stack. This should be removed and cleaned. See fig. 2k.

(5) Drain off coolant into a bucket.

(6) Unscrew the 2 end cap retaining bolts (one each end of the tube stack). Remove the 'O' rings and pull out tube stack. Clean tube stack and end caps.

(7) Re-assemble using new 'O' rings. Do not overtighten end cap bolts and make sure the tube stack is the right way round.

(8) Re-fill engine with water/anti-freeze solution and run engine up to temperature to check for leaks.

Zinc Anode   *Fig. 2j*

Fig. 2k

BELT TENSION

40 AMP ALTERNATOR

WARNING

Belt tension must only be checked with the engine switched off.

(1) The Mini Series range of engines are normally fitted with a single belt to drive the 40 amp battery charging alternator and the fresh water circulating pump.

(2) The belt tension is adjusted by swinging the alternator outboard as it pivots on its power support bolt.

(3) With the engine stopped, loosen the support bolts and the link adjusting bolt.

(4) Push alternator outboard to tension and tighten link bolt.

Check that the depression of the belt at position shown is approximately $1/2$" or 12 mm when pushed down firmly by thumb. Tighten support bolts.

(5) Belt tension should be regularly checked especially during the first 20 hours of running in a new belt, as stretching occurs.

65 AMP ALTERNATOR (OPTION)

The same method, as outlined above applies, but final tensioning must be by hand only. Over tensioning will cause premature failure of components

Link adjust bolt

Support bolt

AIR INTAKE FILTER

These engines are fitted with an air intake filter which should be checked every season and changed every 2 years or sooner if badly clogged.

1

2

3

MAINTENANCE - ELECTRICAL

WARNING ⚠

Under **NO** circumstances should the battery be disconnected or switched off when the engine is running. This will seriously damage the alternator

PANELS AND WIRING

See installation notes, page 32.

GENERAL MAINTENANCE

(1) The panel must be protected from rain and sea water, see installation. Sea water entering the key switch will eventually cause corrosion and could result in the starter motor being permanently energised and burning out. Spray key switch every month with WD 40 or equivalent.

(2) Check batteries for acid level and top up if required. For low maintenance and 'gel' batteries see manufacturers instructions.

(3) Loose spade terminal connections are the most common cause for electrical faults - check on a regular bases (see maintenance instructions).

WINTERISING AND LAYING UP

HEAT EXCHANGER COOLED ENGINES LEFT AFLOAT AND ASHORE

(a) The engine oil and oil filter should be changed at the end of the season rather than in the spring. See section 2.

(b) The closed circuit system should contain a 50/50 solution of anti-freeze (this also applies to warm and tropical climates). Antifreeze should be Ethylene Glycl based conforming to BS6580:1992.

(c) For cold climates where the air or water temperatures can fall below 3°C, the sea water circuit must be protected in addition to the fresh water system. This is best achieved as follows:

(i) Close the inlet seacock to the engine (engine stopped).

(ii) Disconnect the sea water inlet pipe and dip it into a small bucket containing 50/50 anti-freeze solution.

(iii) Start the engine (out of gear) and run for 5 to 10 seconds until the anti-freeze is used up and can be seen coming out of the exhaust outlet.

(iv) Shut engine off and reconnect the inlet pipe to the seacock.

The sea water or raw water circuit is now protected by anti-freeze.

(d) Ensure instrument panel is well protected and give the key switch a spray of WD 40 or equivalent.

(e) With the engine stopped, disconnect the battery (always disconnect the negative cable first and re-connect the negative cable last) and take it ashore for trickle charging and top up as necessary. If AC power is available then this can be done on the boat.

(f) Fuel tanks should be kept full during the lay up period to eliminate water condensation in the tank. Water entering the fuel injection system can cause considerable damage.

LAYING UP ASHORE

(a) Change the engine oil before the boat is taken out of the water.

Warm engine oil is much easier to pump than cold!

(b) to (f) should be followed as above.

LAYING UP CANAL BOATS WITH KEEL COOLING

Follow items a, b, d, e and f. Item (c) does not apply. Special care must be taken to ensure that the whole cooling system has a 30% anti-freeze solution and this includes the calorifier circuit.

If the system has been topped up or refilled then run the engine for 10 to 15 minutes on load (if possible) to get the solution circulated throughout the cooler and calorifier.

TROUBLE SHOOTING

Beta diesels are very reliable if installed and serviced correctly, but problems can occur and the following list gives the most common ones and their solution.

PROBLEM ENGINE DOES NOT START BUT STARTER MOTOR TURNS OVER OK

Possible Cause	Solution
No fuel:	Turn fuel cock on and fill tank.
Air in fuel system:	Vent air (see initial start-up)
Water in fuel:	Change fuel filter and bleed system.
Blocked fuel pipe:	Clean out and bleed system.
Fuel filter clogged:	Change filter and bleed system.
Fuel lift pump blocked:	Remove and replace.
Blocked injector:	Remove and clean.
Fuel return not fed back to the tank:	Re-route fuel return pipe.
Heater plugs not working:	Check wiring to the plugs, and replace plugs if they are burnt out.
Stop solenoid stuck in off position.	Check solenoid is free to return to run position.

PROBLEM: STARTER MOTOR WILL NOT TURN OR TURNS OVER VERY SLOWLY

Possible Cause	Solution
Battery discharged:	Charge battery or replace. Check alternator belt tension.
Starter motor flooded with sea water:	Remove and clean or replace.
Wiring disconnected or loose:	Check circuit for loose connections.
Water in cylinders:	Incorrect installation. This is serious - check engine oil for signs of water (creamy-coloured oil). Ring your dealer.
Engine harness fuse blown:	Replace fuse (located by starter motor or above flywheel housing) and check for wiring faults

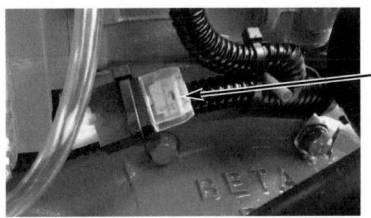

FUSE

Note: For convenience, some engines are supplied with a spare fuse and holder attached onto the main engine fuse holder.

PROBLEM: ERRATIC RUNNING

Possible Cause	Solution
Air in fuel supply:	Check supply system for leaks and fix.
Fuel lift pump faulty:	Replace.
Clogged fuel filter:	Replace.
Fuel return not fed back to the fuel tank, or blocked pipe:	Re-route pipe or clean.
Air filter blocked:	Replace.
Worn or blocked injector:	Service injectors.
Engine rpm in gear is too low, this must be 850 min:	Increase engine tick over speed.
Faulty stop solenoid:	Disconnect wiring to solenoid. If running improves check for a wiring fault.
Broken fuel injection pump spring:	Replace.

PROBLEM: WHITE OR BLUE EXHAUST GAS

Possible Cause	Solution
Engine oil level too high:	Reduce the level.
Blocked injector:	Service injectors.
Piston ring and bore worn, giving a low compression:	Get compression checked by your dealer or Kubota service agent. He will advise action to be taken.
Check that the breather pipe is clear and not obstructed:	Remove and clean out.

PROBLEM: BLACK EXHAUST GAS

Possible Cause	Solution
Blocked air filter element	Inspect and replace
Over pitched propeller - engine will not reach its full rpm:	Check that the engine will reach full rpm in neutral; if it does get the propeller checked / re-pitched if necessary.
Accumulated debris on hull	Inspect and clean if required

PROBLEM: LOW POWER OUTPUT

Possible Cause	Solution
Propeller is too big:	Change or depitch.
Check gearbox reduction ratio relative to propeller size:	Change.

PROBLEM: LOW POWER OUTPUT

Possible Cause	Solution
Blocked fuel filter:	Replace.
Blocked air filter:	Replace.
Air in fuel system:	Check system.
Governor spring incorrectly mounted:	Dealer to adjust.
Single lever control not operating correctly:	Disconnect speed control cable and move the lever by hand. Adjust cable.
The electrical load is too large on start up.	Disconnect or reduce the load.

PROBLEM: HIGH OIL CONSUMPTION

Possible Cause	Solution
Oil leaks:	Check for leaks.
Piston rings worn:	Overhaul required.
Valve stem and guide worn:	Overhaul required.
Piston rings gap facing the same direction:	Shift ring gap position.

PROBLEM: WATER IN LUBRICATING OIL - (Heat exchanger cooled)

Possible Cause	Solution
Oil goes "milky" due to sea water entering exhaust manifold and then into the sump:	Check installation - has anti-siphon valve been fitted? Change engine oil and run engine for 10 minutes each time to eliminate any water. Get fuel injection pump and compression checked by Service Agent.

PROBLEM: WATER IN LUBRICATING OIL - (General)

Possible Cause	Solution
Core plug pushed out due to frozen block:	Service Agent to check and replace.
Water pump seal damaged	Service Agent to check and replace.

PROBLEM: WATER IN LUBRICATING OIL - (Keel cooled)

Possible Cause	Solution
Oil goes "milky" due to water entering exhaust manifold and then into the sump:	Check installation – has dry exhaust system been fitted correctly, ensuring rain water cannot enter the exhaust port and run back? (See DRY EXHAUST SYSTEM) Change engine oil and run engine for 10 minutes each time to eliminate any water. Get fuel injection pump checked by Service Agent.

PROBLEM: LOW OIL PRESSURE WARNING LIGHT comes on when engine speed reduced to tick over:

Possible Cause	Solution
Faulty switch sender:	Replace.
Engine running too hot:	Check cooling water flow (see section 2 Cooling).
Oil relief valve stuck partially open with dirt:	Remove and clean.
Blocked oil filter:	Change.
Wiring fault:	Check circuit.
Insufficient oil:	Top up and check for leaks.

PROBLEM: PANEL REV COUNTER NOT WORKING (WHEN FITTED

Possible Cause	Solution
No W connection to alternator.	Check power output from 'W' connection. Should be about 9V AC.
Wiring fault:	Check circuit.

PROBLEM: ENGINE OVERHEATS

Possible Cause	Solution
Check coolant level:	Top up.
Insufficient sea water flow:	Clear blocked intake or filter.
Damaged or worn pump impeller:	Replace.
Blocked tube stack in heat exchanger:	Remove tube stack and clean - replace 'O' rings.
Zinc anode flakes blocking tube stack:	Remove and clean tube stack as above.
Pressure cap loose:	Replace.
Switch sender faulty:	Replace.
Inlet sea cock is too small:	Replace (see heat exchanger cooled seawater inlet system in section 3).
High exhaust back pressure:	Must not exceed 3.1" of Hg.
Air locks in cooling pipe work to keel cooler:	Vent the system and top up coolant.
Keel cooler of insufficient size:	Contact boat builder.

GENERAL - HEAT EXCHANGE ONLY:

The most common cause of overheating is insufficient seawater flow due to a blocked intake (weed or a plastic bag!). If this happens then clear the blockage. If the problem is not cured then check the system for sea water flow which should be 6.5 litres / minute minimum at 1,000 rpm as follows:

(a) With the boat tied up and out of gear run the engine up to 1000 rpm. *Hold a plastic bucket over the exhaust outlet for 10 seconds and measure the amount of water collected. Multiply this value by 6 to give the flow in litres/min. Repeat twice and take an average. If the flow rate is noticably less than the 6.5 litre per minute minimum, then:

(b) Check impeller in sea water pump - if worn replace.

(c) If impeller has a vane missing then this will be lodged either in the pipe to the heat exchanger or in the end of the exchanger. This must be removed.

(d) Check flow again as in (a).

***Note**: This operation must only be done in safe conditions, in port and with two assistants.

Working from a rubber dinghy is best. The person holding the bucket should take precautions against breathing in the exhaust gasses.

PROBLEM: KNOCKING NOISE

Possible Cause	Solution
Propshaft touching gearbox output coupling through split boss or Type 16 coupling:	Adjust, giving correct clearance (10mm) between gearbox and propeller shaft.
Flexible mount stud touching engine bed:	Adjust stud to clear.
Drive plate broken:	Replace / repair.
Engine touching engine bed:	Re-align engine / modify bed.

PROBLEM: BATTERY QUICKLY DISCHARGES

Possible Cause	Solution
High load and insufficient running:	Reduce load or increase charging time. Large domestic battery banks subject to high electrical loads will take a considerable time to recharge from a single alternator.
Low electrolyte level:	Top up.
Fan belt slipping - black dust in engine compartment: Engine compartment temperature too high.	Adjust tension / replace belt with a high temperature and/or improve engine box ventilation.
Alternator defective:	Check with Agent.
Battery defective:	Replace.
Poor wiring connection:	Check wiring system.

PROBLEM: TRANSMISSION NOISE

Possible Cause	Solution
Check gearbox oil level:	Top up.
"Singing" propeller:	Check with supplier.
Drive plate rattle at tickover:	Check engine rpm (must be 850 rpm minimum in gear).
Worn drive plate:	Change.
Propellor shaft hitting the gearbox half coupling	Move shaft back to give at least 5mm clearance (type 12/16 couplings only)

PROBLEM: VIBRATION

Possible Cause	Solution
Poor alignment to shaft:	The alignment must be accurate even if a flexible coupling is used (see section 3 ALIGNMENT).
Flexible mounts not adjusted correctly to take even weight:	Check relative compression of each mount.
Flexible mount rubber perished:	Replace. (Diesel or oil will eventually perish most rubbers.)
Loose securing nut on flexible mount:	Check alignment and then tighten the nuts.
Insufficient clearance between the propeller tip and the bottom of the boat:	There must be at least 10% tip clearance between propeller and bottom of the boat (ie 10% of the propeller diameter as clearance). Refer to boatbuilder.
Loose zinc anode on the shaft:	Tighten or replace.
Worn cutless bearing or shaft:	Replace.
Weak engine support/bearers:	Check for cracked or broken feet.

PROBLEM: MORSE CONTROL CABLE WILL NOT FIT

Possible Cause	Solution
Fitting incorrectly	Cables are being fitted the wrong way around, switch over and fit the opposite way.

ELECTRICAL FAULT FINDING & TROUBLE SHOOTING – ENGINES BUILT AFTER JULY 2005 ONLY

The following chart is compiled to aid diagnosis of electrical faults, based on the Beta 10-90hp range of engines. If your engine was built before July 2005, contact Beta Marine for the relevant electrical trouble shooting guide.

Standard sea specification engines (heat exchanger cooled) are supplied with a single alternator, mounted port side, supplying power to starter battery and control panel.

Standard canal specification engines (keel cooled) are supplied with twin alternators:

- 1st alternator, mounted port side, supplying power to starter battery and control panel
- 2nd alternator, the standard mounting position for this is above the engine on the starboard side (or below 1st alternator on 75 & 90hp), supplying power to the domestic battery system.

Both of these alternators work independently, if the domestic battery system is disconnected, the engine will still run correctly but:

- Domestic charge warning lamp will not function
- Warning buzzer will remain on at all times

Standard control panels are supplied with four or five lamps:

Four lamp panels:
A, ABV, ABVW, B these panels utilise bulbs inside sealed lamp holders

Five lamp panels:
AB and C, these panels also utilise bulbs inside sealed lamp holders, having an additional lamp for domestic battery charge

With keyswitch* in run position & engine off:

- Red lamp for no starter battery charge should function
- Red lamp for no domestic battery charge should function (Note: this will only function if a second alternator is fitted to the engine and connected to a charged battery)

All Beta panels have the following warning lamps: (A, AB, ABV, ABVW, B and C Deluxe)

Starter battery charge warning lamp		Red
• High engine temperature warning lamp		Red
• Low engine oil pressure warning lamp		Red

All panels also have:

• Panel power on (this is not a warning lamp)		Green

In addition to above the domestic AB, C Deluxe panels also have a:

• Domestic battery charge warning lamp		Red

- Red lamp for high engine temperature should not function (when engine is cold / cool / warm). This lamp will only ever function if the engine is over temperature.
- Red lamp for low oil pressure should function
- Green lamp for panel power on should function
- Buzzer should sound

For operation of engines controlled with keyless panels refer to 'correct operation of keyless panels' later in this section

When the engine is started, all the red warning lamps should switch off leaving just the green power on indication lamp illuminated. The oil pressure lamp may take a few seconds to switch off and the charge fail lamp may remain on until engine rpm is increased to approximately 1,000rpm if the engine was started at tickover).

Before investigating any specific electrical problem, always check:

- Connection between panel harness and panel loom. It must be clean, dry and secured with a cable tie.
- Check the start battery is connected to the correct terminal on the starter motor.
- Check the domestic battery is switched on and connected to the correct terminals for the 2nd alternator.
- Battery connections, inspecting condition of cables from battery to engine. If in doubt measure the voltage at the engine.
- If alternator charge problem, measure battery voltage with engine off and again with engine running, if there is an increase alternator is functioning correctly, if not refer to check list.

Note: The two way plug on panel loom will only have a corresponding socket to connect into from the engine if a 2nd alternator is fitted which requires this connection. Engines with only one alternator do not utilise this connection.

Typical start battery positive

Typical start battery negative

ELECTRICAL FAULT FINDING – LED PANELS

PROBLEM	POSSIBLE CAUSE & SOLUTION
No warning lamps or buzzer functioning, engine will not start or stop	• Battery isolation switch in off position –switch on • Starter battery discharged – charge • Engine fuse blown –check fuse (above starter motor or flywheel housing) & replace if necessary. • Check for wiring faults.
Non function of warning lamp **THE WATER TEMPERATURE LAMP WILL NOT FUNCTION UNLESS ENGINE IS OVERHEATING OR THERE IS A WIRING FAULT**	• Disconnect switch wire to non-functioning lamp: green/blue –water temperature, white/brown –oil pressure, brown/yellow –alternator charge. Reconnect wire temporarily to another warning lamp that is functioning; if wire switches lamp on replace faulty lamp. • Disconnect positive feed to non-functioning lamp. Reconnect temporarily with wire from another warning lamp that is functioning, if wire switches lamp on rewire with new connection. • If none of the above, check continuity of connections from panel to engine.
Water temperature warning Lamp on when engine is not over temperature (Not B or C deluxe panel see table on following page)	**If engine is cold:** • Faulty wiring, check connection & continuity (small green / blue) from switch to panel lamp. Ensure this connection is not shorting to earth (ground). • Faulty temperature switch –if lamp switches off on removal of connection to switch unit, replace. **If engine is warm:** • Switch wire connected to large sender terminal of switch / sender unit. Remove and refit to smaller (switch) terminal
Buzzer not functioning **THE BUZZER WILL NOT SOUND FOR GREEN POWER ON LAMP**	• - If lamp is functioning but buzzer not sounding, check connection & continuity from illuminated warning lamp (red not green) to buzzer board. • - Faulty warning panel buzzer board –replace.
Starter battery charge lamp not functioning	• If tacho not functioning: • Alternator not connected properly, check continuity of small brown wire from rear of alternator to 'AC' position on keyswitch. • alternator connected properly, faulty alternator –replace • If tacho functioning correctly: • Check continuity of small brown/yellow wire from rear of alternator to no charge warning lamp on rear of panel. • If alternator connected properly, faulty panel warning lamp –replace
Tacho not functioning	• -Check connections on rear of tacho, especially black/blue wire, terminal '4' • -Check connection of black/blue wire on rear of 1st alternator (W connection, usually a bullet on flying lead, or lowest connection on alternators with 3 pin coupler) • -Check continuity of black/blue wire from alternator to tacho • -Measure voltage from alternator W connection to earth (ground), should be approx. 7.5 – 9.0 volts AC
Domestic charge lamp not functioning, buzzer remains on with engine running	• Domestic battery not connected • Domestic battery not connected correctly: B+ to domestic isolation block on starboard rail (port on 75 & 95hp) B- to engine earth (ground) • Domestic battery flat • Panel relay faulty / incorrectly wired: Check voltage at relay terminal 86, white wire is positive feed for warning lamp from AC position of keyswitch.
Domestic charge lamp not functioning, buzzer switching off with engine running **THIS LAMP WILL NOT FUNCTION IF A SINGLE ALTERNATOR IS FITTED TO THE ENGINE**	• No second alternator fitted to engine, domestic lamp not used • D+ (charge indication) lamp connection at rear of alternator not connected • Two way plug & socket disconnected between engine harness & panel loom

ELECTRICAL FAULT FINDING – C DELUXE & WATER TEMPERATURE FUNCTION ON B PANELS

In addition to the fault finding detailed on the previous table, the following is specific for the C Deluxe type deluxe panel (Also applicable for the B panel with Murphy water temperature gauge)

PROBLEM	POSSIBLE CAUSE & SOLUTION
Oil pressure warning lamp not functioning, oil pressure gauge showing maximum deflection. Engine off and keyswitch in run position	• Faulty wiring –check wire connection & continuity (small white/brown) from sender to panel lamp. Ensure this connection is not shorting to earth (ground).
Oil pressure gauge showing no movement - even when engine is started. Warning lamp functioning correctly	• Faulty wiring –check oil pressure sender wire (small white / brown) is connected.
Oil pressure showing no movement, Warning lamp not functioning correctly	• Check connection to oil pressure gauge, if plug is not connected to socket on rear of gauge reconnect. • If all connections are correctly made, possible faulty sender unit –check resistance to earth (ground) approx. 50W. Replace if no reading or short-circuited. • If adjusted correctly & buzzer still sounding, possible faulty switch gauge unit – replace.
Oil pressure showing normal operating pressure (0.75–5 bar). Buzzer sounding & lamp illuminated.	**Engine warm:** • Incorrectly calibrated switching point for warning lamp, adjust on rear of gauge to 0.5 bar (minimum adjustment on gauge). • If adjusted correctly & buzzer still sounding, faulty switch gauge unit – replace.
Water temperature gauge showing 120°C / 250°F **THIS ALSO APPLIES TO THE B PANEL WITH MURPHY GAUGE**	**Engine cold / cool:** • Faulty wiring, check water temperature sender wire is not shorting to earth • Faulty sender unit, –check resistance to earth, approx. $3.5k\Omega$ (cold) – $0.5k\Omega$ (warm). Replace if notably less.
Water temperature gauge showing normal operating temperature (85°C). Buzzer sounding & lamp illuminated. **THIS ALSO APPLIES TO THE B PANEL WITH MURPHY GAUGE**	**Engine warm:** • Incorrectly calibrated switching point for warning lamp, adjust on rear of gauge to 100°C. • If adjusted correctly & buzzer still sounding, faulty switch gauge unit – replace.
Water temperature gauge showing no movement, LED not illuminated, engine warm.	• Check connection to sender, if disconnected gauge will not function. • Check connection to temperature gauge, if plug is not connected to socket on rear of gauge reconnect. • If all connections are correctly made, faulty sender unit –check resistance to earth, approx. $3.5k\Omega$ (cold) – $0.5k\Omega$ (warm). Replace if no reading.

ELECTRICAL – CORRECT OPERATION OF KEYLESS PANELS

These panels control the engine with three water resistant push buttons instead of a keyswitch, which are less prone to damage and corrosion from sea water spray than a keyswitch.
To operate the engine:
1. Press and hold 'HEAT' button for ten seconds maximum
- Red lamp for no starter battery charge should function
- Red lamp for high engine temperature should not function (when engine is cold / cool / warm). This lamp will only ever function if the engine is over temperature.
- Red lamp for low oil pressure should function

- Green lamp for panel power on should function
- Buzzer should sound
2. Press 'START' button and hold in position until engine fires (see initial start-up section for maximum time starter can be operated). Release button (when engine has started)
- All red warning lamps should extinguish and buzzer should stop sounding. The oil pressure lamp may take a few seconds to switch off and the charge fail lamp may remain on until engine rpm is increased to approximately 1,000rpm if the engine was started at tickover.

- Green lamp for panel power on should still function
3. To stop the engine press the 'STOP' push button, hold in until engine stops. This button also switches the power off to the gauges, engine and power on lamp.
4. To re-start the engine, simply repeat steps from '1' above, there is no need to switch battery isolators off whilst remaining on board.
5. If leaving the boat, isolate start battery from engine and panel, to prevent accidental start up of engine.

ELECTRICAL FAULT FINDING – NON BETA PANELS

Engines can be supplied wired up to suit VDO switch senders, usually fitted to a non-Beta control panel.

If so refer to our wiring diagram 200-60971/01 (also part number for replacement harness)

- Loom is configured differently in the 11-way plug to accommodate the extra wiring.
- Small brown wire (battery sensed alternator feed) fitted with bullet connection beside harness plug.
- Oil pressure & water temperature switch / senders fitted to engine, requiring individual connections for driving gauges & warning lamps.

Note: Water temperature switch / sender
- large spade is sender connection
- small spade is switch connection

Oil pressure switch / sender
- G   Gauge wire
- M   Earth
- WK Warning lamp

(Part number 200-01133)
(green / blue)
(blue / yellow)

(Part number 200-62680)
(white / brown)
(black)
(green / yellow)

ELECTRICAL FAULT FINDING – EXTENSION HARNESSES

Some installations require one of the panel extensions 11 way connectors to be removed to allow the cable to be passed through bulkheads etc. If any panel problems are experienced after this may have been carried out, visually check all 11 way connections on engine harness to panel extension (and panel extension to panel on C deluxe) to ensure wire colours to each terminal match up to the correct colour in its corresponding terminal. Extra attention must be given to black (ground) and black/blue (tacho), also brown (switched positive to alternator) and brown/yellow (charge fail) as these connections are harder to distinguish between in poorly lit areas. Whilst doing this check integrity of each connection to ensure terminals have not become damaged. Once checked, re-fit cable tie around each connection to keep them secure.

BETA PART NUMBERS FOR REPLACEMENT ITEMS:

Description	Part number
40 amp blade fuse (all panels)	200-00959
Alarm board –all panels from June 05	200-04655
Oil pressure switch 1/8"BSP (not C panels)	600-62670
Oil pressure sender (C panels only)	200-94350
Oil pressure switch gauge (C panels only)	200-96190
Temperature switch with single terminal (on some Beta 16 & Beta 25)	600-62820
Temperature switch / sender 1/8"BSP (not B or C panels)	200-01133
Temperature sender (B & C panels only)	200-94360
Water temperature switch gauge (B & C panels only)	200-96200
Voltmeter (C panels only)	200-96210
28Ra relay 12V 40A (fitted to rear of domestic panels)	200-87020
Keyswitch, silver bezel	600-00057
Panel stop button (all panels) –Also heat and start on ABVW	200-00072
Tacho, 0-4000rpm with digital hour counter (all panels but A)	200-02373
Standard engine harness Mini Series	200-98380/01
Standard engine harness S5 Series	200-60973/05
Standard engine harness S3 series	200-05267
Iskra 65 amp sub loom	200-01196
1m panel extension loom	200-04588/01
2m panel extension loom	200-04588/02
3m panel extension loom	200-04588/03
4m panel extension loom	200-04588/04
Domestic charge engine sub loom (top mounted alternators)	200-01197
Green power on indicator lamp & retaining clip	200-04656
Red warning indicator lamp & retaining clip	200-04657

Note: the above part numbers are suitable for earth return installations only (where battery negative cable is connected directly to engine ground). For insulated earth (where battery negative cable is isolated from engine ground) different harnesses, alternators, switches for oil pressure and engine temperature will be required. If your application is wired as insulated earth return and the engine will not operate correctly, always check starter battery negative is connected to the correct terminal on the isolating solenoid. It should be connected to the terminal which is also used for all the small black wires, **NOT the terminal with the single black wire connected directly to engine ground.**

Spanner torque settings

Tightening Torques for general use bolts and nuts

ITEM	Size x Pitch	kgf·m	ft·lbs	N·m
M6 (7T) : 6mm (0.24in)	–	1.0~1.15	7.2~8.3	9.8~11.3
M8 (7T) : 8mm (0.31)	–	2.4~2.8	17.4~20.3	23.5~27.5
M10 (7T) : 10mm (0.39in)	–	5.0~5.7	36.2~41.2	49.0~55.9
M12 (7T) : 12mm (0.47in)	–	7.9~9.2	57.1~66.5	77.5~90.5

Tightening Torques for special use bolts and nuts

Head Bolts	M8 x 1.25	3.8~4.3	27.5~31.1	37.3~42.2
Bolts, Connecting Bolts	M7 x 0.75	2.7~3.1	19.5~22.4	26.5~30.4
Bolts, Flywheel	M10 x 1.25	5.5~6.0	39.8~43.4	53.9~58.8
Bolts 1, Bearing Case	M6 x 1.0	1.3~1.6	9.4~11.6	12.7~15.7
Bolts 2, Bearing Case	M7 x 1.0	2.7-3.1	19.5~22.4	26.5~30.4
Nozzle Holder Assembly	M20 x 1.5	5.0~7.0	36.2~50.6	49.0~68.6
Caps Nuts, Head Cover	M6 x 1.0	0.4~0.6	2.9~4.3	3.9~5.9
Glow Plugs	M8~1.0	0.8~1.5	5.8~10.8	7.8~14.7
Oil Switch	PT 1/8	1.5~2.0	10.8~14.5	14.7~19.6
Nuts, Rocker Arm Bracket	M6 x 1.0	1.0~1.15	7.2~8.3	9.8~11.3
Bolts, Idle Gear Shaft	M6 x 1.0	1.0~1.15	7.2~8.3	9.8~11.3

Section 3

INSTALLATION RECOMMENDATIONS

The installation details contained herewith are basic guidelines to assist installation, due to great diversity of marine craft it is impossible to give definitive instructions. Therefore Beta Marine can accept no responsibility for any damage or injury incurred during the installation of a Beta Marine Engine whilst following these guidelines.

- All engines shall be placed within an enclosure separated from living quarters and installed so as to minimise the risk of fires or spread of fires as well as hazards from toxic fumes, heat, noise or vibrations in the living quarters.

- Unless the engine is protected by a cover or its own enclosure, exposed moving or hot parts of the engine that could cause personal injury shall be effectively shielded.

- Engine parts and accessories that require frequent inspection and / or servicing must be readily accessible.

- The insulating materials inside engine spaces shall be not combustible.

ENGINE MOUNTING

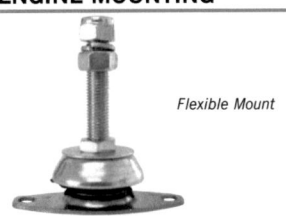

Flexible Mount

WARNING ⚠

1. Do not set the engine feet high up the flexible mount pillar stud. This will cause excessive engine movement and vibration. Pack under the flexible mount with steel shims securely bolted into the engine bearer.

2. The pillar stud on the flexible mount is secured into position by the lower locknut, do not forget to tighten this. Also ensure that the stud is not screwed too far through the mounting body so that it can touch the bearer. This will cause vibration and knocking noises which are very hard to find!!

To ensure vibration free operation, the engine must be installed on substantial beds, extending as far forward and aft as possible and well braced to form an integral part of the hull.

The engine must be installed as low as possible on the flexible mount pillar stud. This will limit vibration and extend the life of the flexible mount. If necessary, fit spacer blocks below the mounts.

A flexible coupling should be fitted. Flexible couplings do not accommodate bad alignment. The mating faces of the gearbox and tailshaft must be checked for alignment, they must be parallel and concentric to within 0.005" (0.127mm).

ALIGNMENT

Alignment must be checked for parallel (A) and concentric (B) misalignment using a set of feeler gauges. To obtain accurate alignment the flexible mountings must be adjusted until alignment is attained, and the mountings must be locked in position. Once mounts are tightened, alignment must be re-checked. Coupling can now be fitted in accordance with instructions supplied with coupling.

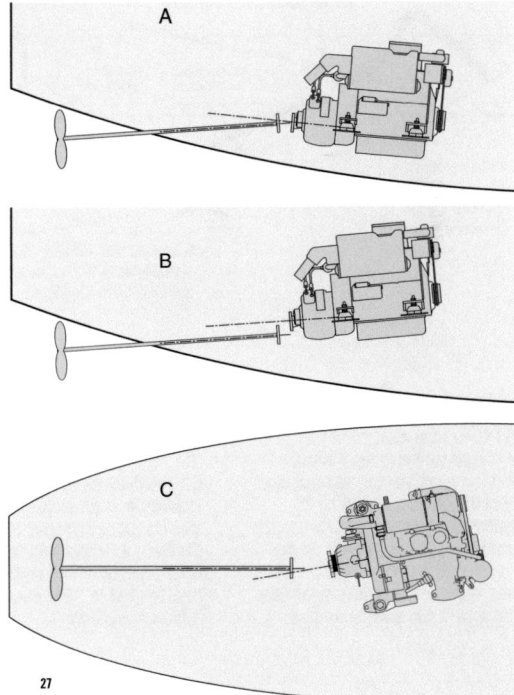

EXHAUSTS

(a) A correctly installed engine as described in this handbook will meet the exhaust emission requirements of Directive 2003/44/EC amending the Recreational Craft Directive 94/25/EC.

(b) For compliance with exhaust emissions requirements, engines must have correctly installed exhaust systems. To ensure exhaust emissions are kept within permissible limits it is most important to reduce exhaust back pressure to a minimum, whilst ensuring exhaust is adequately muffled. Back pressure increases as exhaust length increases and from bends in the exhaust system. The exhaust back pressure, measured with the exhaust system connected and the engine running at full speed, must not exceed 80mmHg (3.1 inches Hg / 42 inches WG). The correct measuring point is at the position where the exhaust connects to the exhaust manifold. That is before the water injection elbow or dry exhaust bellows.

Wet Exhaust hose should be matched to the injection bend sizes detailed above.

Exhausts	Beta 10	BZ482 / Beta 16	BD722 / Beta 25
Standard	50mm	50mm	50mm
Option 1⅝" is available in SS	1⅝"	1⅝"	1⅝"
High rise water injection bend SS	50mm	50mm	50mm
Cross over injection bend SS to suit Volvo replacement engines.	50mm	50mm	50mm

TYPICAL YACHT INSTALLATION

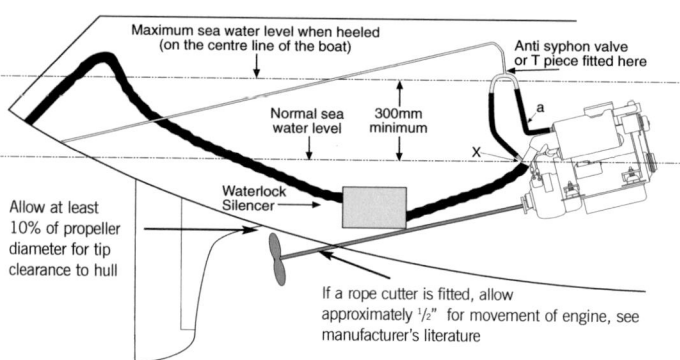

WARNING:

(1) One of the most common problems with engine installation is water entering the exhaust manifold from the exhaust system by syphoning. This can occur when the point of water injection (X) on the engine is close to or below the water line. Water entering the pistons can cause bent con rods, emulsified engine oil and a wrecked fuel pump! Its best avoided!

(2) The diagram shows a typical installation. It is essential that the small black rubber hose connecting the heat exchanger with the injection bend is removed and replaced by a hose marked 'a'. This must be of sufficient length to supply either a T piece or an anti syphon valve sited at least 300mm (12 inches) above the water line and on the centre line of the boat. The pipe then returns to the injection bend and the sea water is pumped down the exhaust pipe.

(3) The exhaust back pressure should not exceed 3.1 inches of Hg.

DRY EXHAUST SYSTEM

The exhaust system installed in a canal boat or work boat with a dry exhaust should be 1½" minimum ID. The engine is fitted with a 1½" BSP male connector when a dry exhaust system is specified. A flexible exhaust bellows and dry exhaust silencer should be used. It is up to the installer to work out his own pipe run but care should be taken as follows:

(1) Ensure that rain water cannot enter the exhaust port and run back down the system, flooding the silencer and eventually the engine.

(2) The system should be lagged if there is any danger of the crew getting near it.

(3) A dry exhaust system will give off considerable heat and suitable ventilation must be provided.

(4) The exhaust back pressure should not exceed 3.1 inches of Hg.

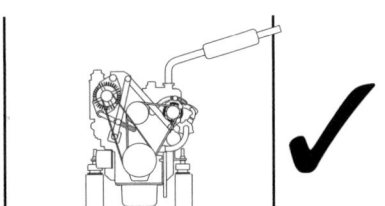
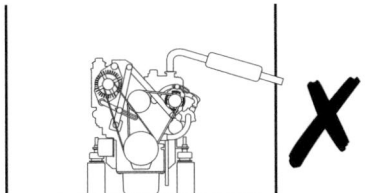

Ensure exhaust raises then falls to outlet

FUEL SUPPLY & LEAK OFF - A typical system is shown below

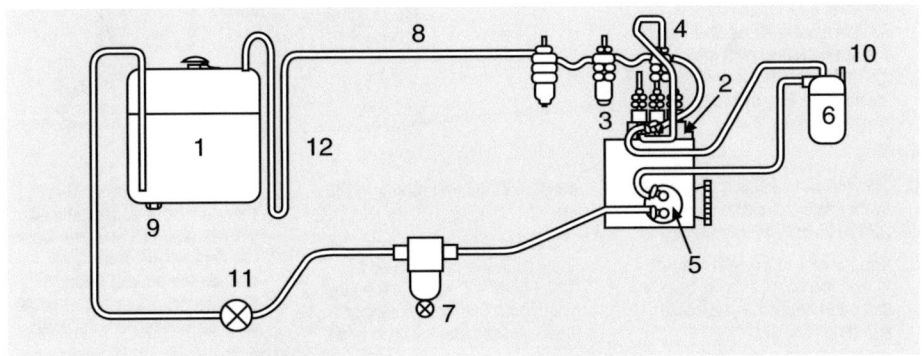

(1) Fuel tank
(2) Injection pump
(3) Injection nozzle
(4) Injection pipe
(5) Mechanical fuel feed pump with priming lever
(6) Fuel filter
(7) Fuel water separator
(8) Overflow/leak off
(9) Drain plug
(10) Air vent
(11) Stop cock
(12) Fuel pipe loop

Notes:

1. The mechanical fuel lift pump is fitted to all engines as standard, but if a suction head of 0.25m is required then an electric fuel lift pump must be fitted (ask your dealer or Beta Marine).

2. It is very important that the excess fuel from the injectors is fed back to the fuel tank and not back to any point on the supply line. This will help prevent air getting into the system.

4. Any fuel leaks in the system are likely to cause poor starting and erratic running and must be corrected immediately.

5. A fuel/water separator must be installed.

6. The fuel return (leak off) pipe must loop down to be level with the bottom of the tank before it enters the top of the tank - see 12. This prevents fuel 'drain down'.

7. Fuel lines and hoses must be secured and separated or protected from any source of significant heat. The filling, storage, venting and fuel supply arrangements and installations must be designed and installed so as to minimise the risk of fire and explosion. Flexible fuel hoses connecting the engine to fuel tank supply and return lines must meet the requirements set in standard ISO 7840:1995/A1:2000 and as required by your surveyor / authority.

3. Fuel pipe sizes are:

	Supply (mm)	Leak off (mm)
Beta 10	8	8
BZ482 / Beta 16	8	8
BD722 / Beta 25	8	8

SEAWATER INLET SYSTEM (HEAT EXCHANGER COOLED ENGINES)

Your engine is fitted with a gear driven sea water pump which sucks in seawater or raw water to cool the closed circuit system via the heat exchanger.

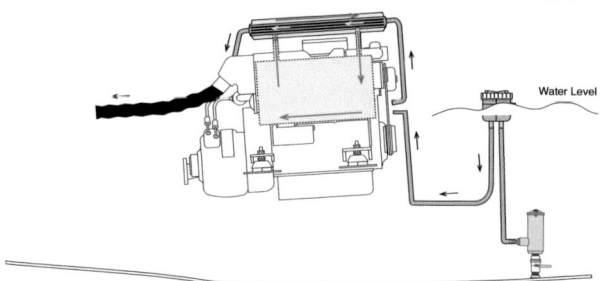

1. It is very important that the seawater inlet should have a strainer system either built into the sea cock or a high level system with visual inspection glass, as shown, mounted just above the water line.

2. The inlet sea cock and pipe work to the sea water pump should be 22mm ID or 3/4" minimum.

3. Good access to the inlet seacock is essential so that plastic bags or sea weed trapped in the intake can be poked out!

4. All pipe work should have approved marine grade stainless steel hose clips. Any loose clamps or bad connections can cause flooding and sinking of the vessel.

5. If water is required for stern tube lubrication then this should be taken from a 'T' piece in the pipe going from the heat exchanger outlet to the water injection bend.

6. Scoop type water pickups should never be used, as water will be forced through the pump and into the exhaust system whilst the vessel is in motion. This is very dangerous as the exhaust will eventually fill and raw water will back up into the engine through the exhaust valve. Catastrophic failure will result as soon as the engine is restarted.

Note: The maximum lift of the sea water pump is 2m

KEEL COOLED

1. The supply pipe to the keel cooler should be 22mm bore and the return 22mm bore.

2. The tank size should have a surface area (x) exposed to the sea water or canal water of (0.25 x the bhp of the engine) = sq ft of cooling area required. For canal boats this should be adequately baffled and a vent provided to expel any air. The supply (hot water) goes in at the top of the tank and the return comes out of the bottom. Also refer to cooling tank notes on page 10.

IDEAL KEEL COOLING TANK

Air bleed valves

BAFFLE

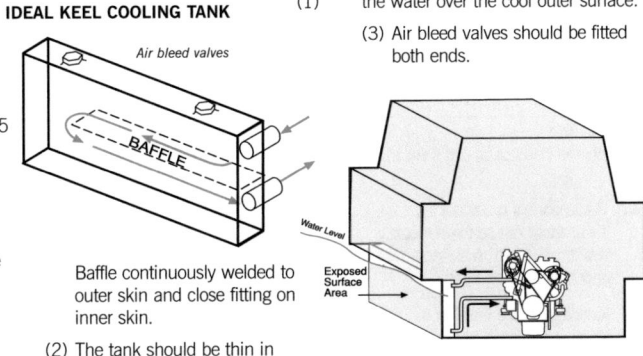

(1) the water over the cool outer surface.

(3) Air bleed valves should be fitted both ends.

Baffle continuously welded to outer skin and close fitting on inner skin.

(2) The tank should be thin in section to allow good mixing of

CALORIFIER SYSTEM

All Beta engines can be fitted with the engine tappings to allow the hot water from the closed fresh water/antifreeze system to circulate through a calorifier tank which in turn heats up domestic water.

Calorifier tappings on this range of engine are shown below.

1. The big problem with a calorifier is to remove all the air from the system. If this is not achieved then they don't work!

2. Try and keep the supply and return pipes a and b either horizontal or sloping down in a continuous fall. This avoids air pockets being created.

3. Extra care must be taken when first filling the calorifier circuit system with 50% antifreeze to water solution as the engine may appear to be full but it soon disappears into the calorifier pipe work. Run the engine off load for 10 minutes then check the level as described in 'Filling The Fresh Water System'.

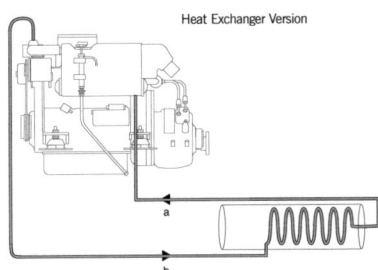

Heat Exchanger Version

Keel Cooled Version

Also check to see if the pipe going to the calorifier is getting warm after 15 minutes. Top up the water level as required and run for another 10 minutes then repeat.

4. If the water level is steady but no warm water is getting to the calorifier then very carefully open the calorifier bleed valve (see manufacturers instructions) or if none is provided then very carefully loosen the jubilee clip securing the supply pipe to the calorifier. Air should escape. Refasten securely when no further bubbles are seen.

CAUTION ⚠

Do not do this when the engine is hot as scalding hot water may be forced out of the pipe under pressure.

ELECTRICAL INSTALLATIONS

Beta has 4 panels:
- A - standard
- AB or ABV or ABVW
- B
- C

The engine harness is common to all.

1. These panels must not be installed where sea water spray can get at them. A suitable flap or cover must be fitted.

2. Panels must be fitted in a location where the helmsman can either see or hear the alarm system.

3. For standard wiring diagrams see following pages.

4. Extension looms longer than 3m (10 feet): As an option, Beta can provide various lengths of extension looms for runs of over 3m, but this kit includes a start relay to overcome the voltage drop. (See drawing 300-58520)

5. All electrical equipment must be protected from sea water. Sea water or rust in the starter will invalidate the warranty. Care must be taken when pushing the two halves of the plug together to ensure that individual pins do not fall out. To prevent corrosion and assist in assembly we recommend that the plug is packed with petroleum jelly (Vaseline) and then carefully pushed together. The plastic boots should cover both halves and overlap. A cable tie is then put around to hold the two halves in position and help prevent any ingression of water.

6. All cables must be adequately clipped and protected from abrasion.

7. Electrical systems shall be designed and installed so as to ensure proper operation of the craft under normal conditions of use and shall be such as to minimise risk of fire and electric shock.

8. Attention shall be paid to the provision of overload and short-circuit protection of all circuits, except engine starting circuits, supplied from batteries.

9. Ventilation shall be provided to prevent the accumulation of gases, which might be emitted from batteries. Batteries shall be firmly secured and protected from ingress of water

APPENDICES – WIRING DIAGRAMS & GENERAL ARRANGEMENTS

1. Keyswitch terminations		Page 33
2. Standard harness	200-05444	Page 34
3. 65 amp harness	200-05495	Page 35
4. Diagram of A panel & cut-out	200-06516	Page 36 & 37
5. Diagram of AB panel & cut-out	200-06517	Page 38 & 39
6. Diagram of ABV panel & cut-out	200-06519	Page 40 & 41
7. Diagram of ABVW panel & cut-out	100-06333	Page 42 & 43
8. Diagram of C panel & cut-out	200-06520	Page 44 & 45
9. Diagram of C Deluxe panel & cut-out	200-06518	Page 46 & 47
10. Blocking diode diagram –40A alt	300-62220	Page 48
11. Split charge diagram –65A alt	300-62210	Page 49
12. Starter booster relay	300-58520	Page 50
13. GA of B10 H/E -TMC40	100-00030	Page 51
14. GA of BZ482 H/E -TMC40	100-06019	Page 52
15. GA of Beta 16 (BZ602) H/E -TMC40	100-06496	Page 53
16. GA of BD722 H/E -TMC40	100-99610	Page 54
17. GA of BD722 H/E -PRM80	100-01048	Page 55
18. GA of BD722 K/C -PRM80	100-05749	Page 56
19. GA of Beta 25 (BD902) H/E –TMC40	100-06495	Page 57
20. GA of Beta 25 (BD902) H/E –PRM120	100-06509	Page 58
21. GA of Beta 25 (BD902) H/E –TTMC35	100-06494	Page 59
22. Declaration of Conformity for Recreational Craft		Page 60
23. Maintenance record and service items		Page 64 & 65

NOTE: for dual battery charging on Beta 16 and Beta 25 models fitted with the optional 60 Amp alternator, a blocking diode arrangement be utilised, refer to 300-62220. This is a battery sensed machine, incompatible with our standard split charge relay.

TYPICAL STARTER MOTOR RATINGS:-

Starters used in Kubota engines have the following standard capacities

Engine	Starter capacity (kW)
Less than 700cc	0.8 to 1.0
700 to 1500cc	1.0 to 1.4

SUGGESTED MINIMUM ENGINE STARTER BATTERY SIZE:

Engine (cc)	Typical Battery Capacity (AH) at a 20hr Rate	Typical C.C.A. (A) Cold Cranking Amperage
Beta 10/BZ482/Beta 16	35~ 40	350~ 405
BD722/Beta 25	65~ 75	450~ 540

KEYSWITCH TERMINATIONS

The standard panel keyswitch can be used to tap off a switched positive ignition feed to power additional gauges. In this way these gauges will only be live whilst the engine is running, the engine is starting or the heaters are being used.

For silver keyswitches, the terminal to achieve this ignition switched positive is marked 'AC'.

For black keyswitches, the terminal to achieve this ignition switched positive is marked '15/54'.

For panels without any keyswitch, gauges can be driven from the $1mm^2$ brown wire which teriminates at 11 way connector terminal 4. This is a lower power switched positive, any additional power required from this connection must be feed through a relay, as noted below.

Note: these keyswitch terminals are rated at 10 amps maximum, since they are already utilised for panel and alternator feeds Beta Marine recommend any additional requirements from these terminals must be fed through a relay. This relay should then be connected to it's own fused positive supply directly from the engine battery.

Beta drawing 202-06421 illustrating the wiring of a typical electric fuel lift pump with ignition switched relay can be supplied upon request.

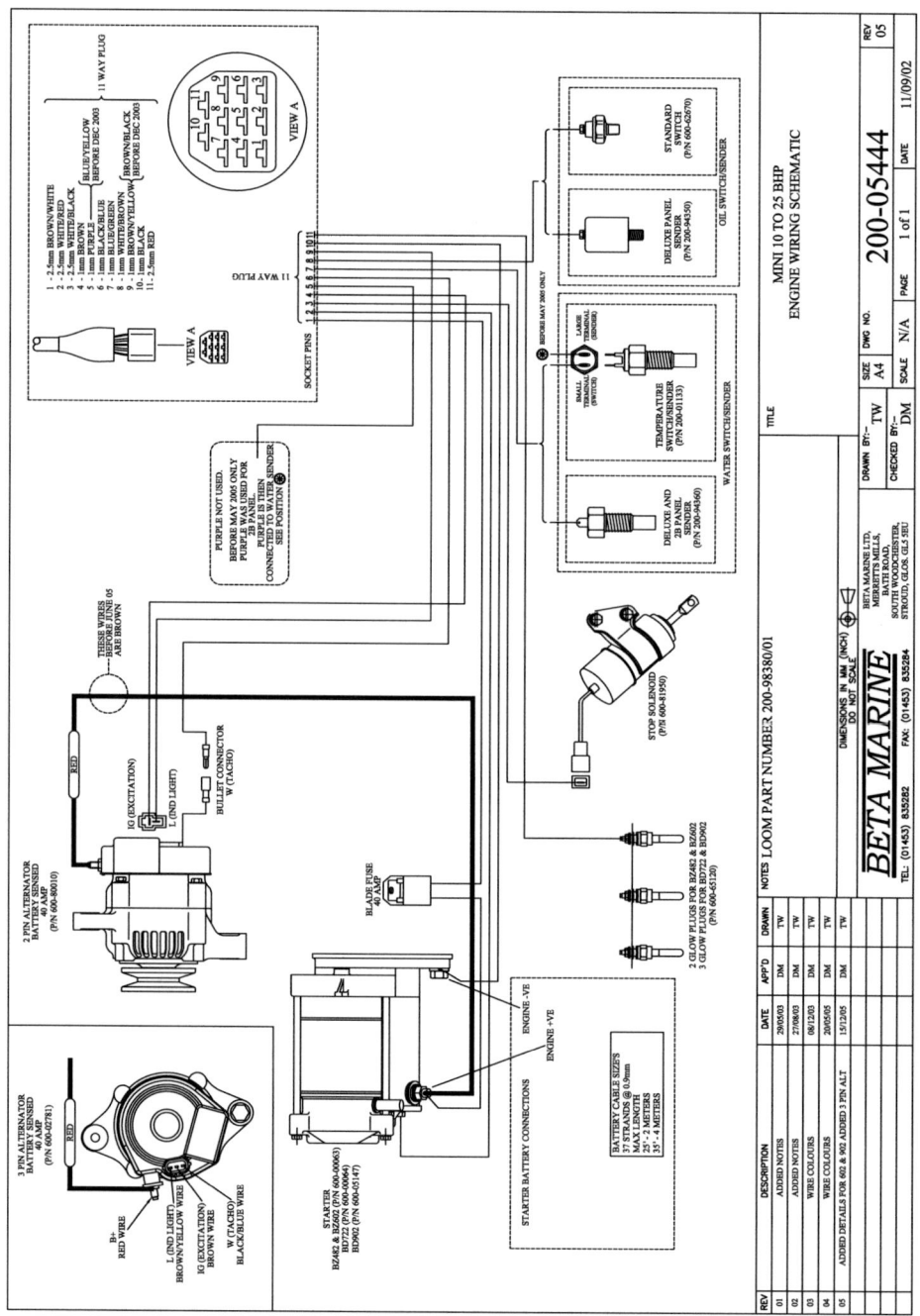

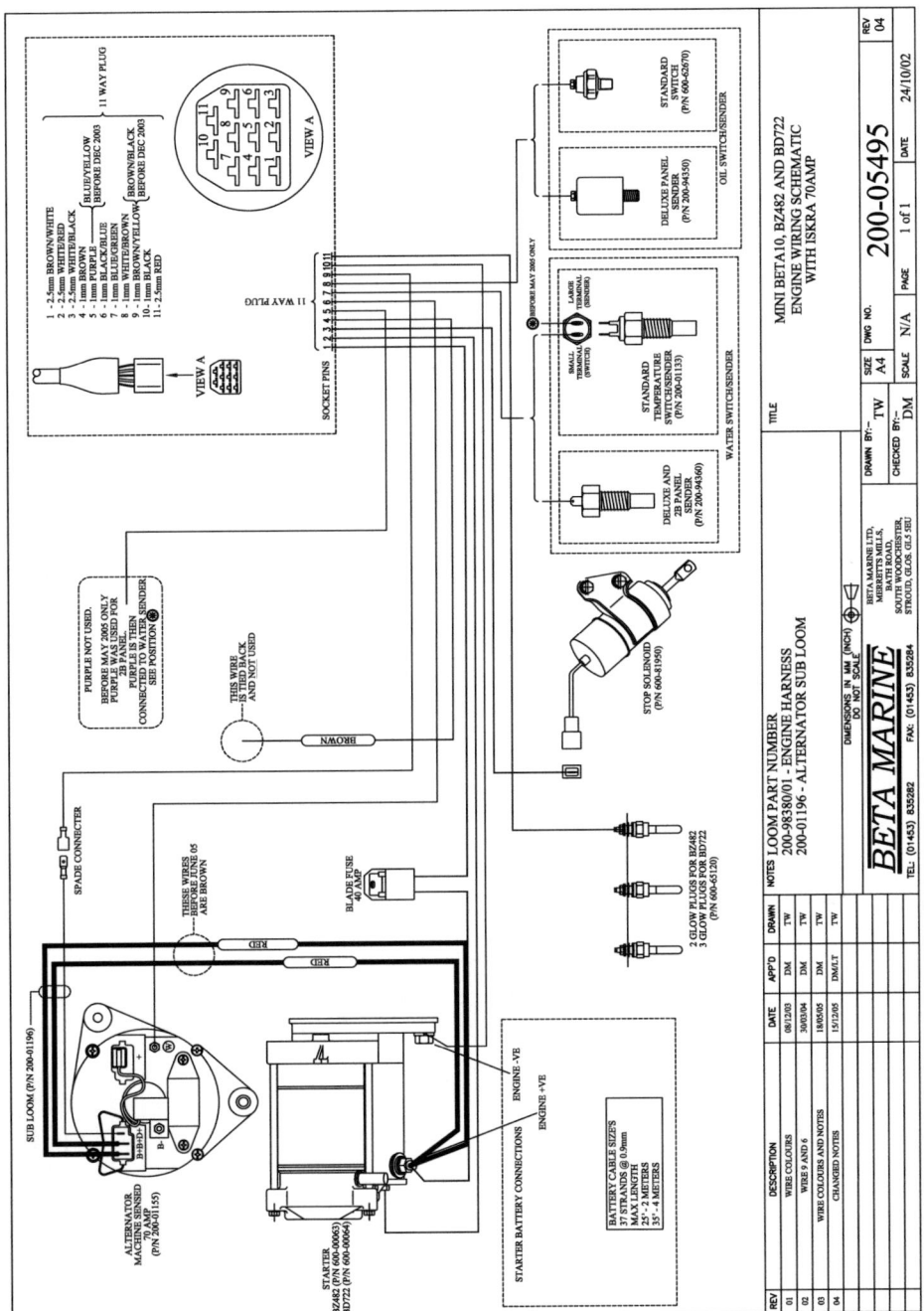

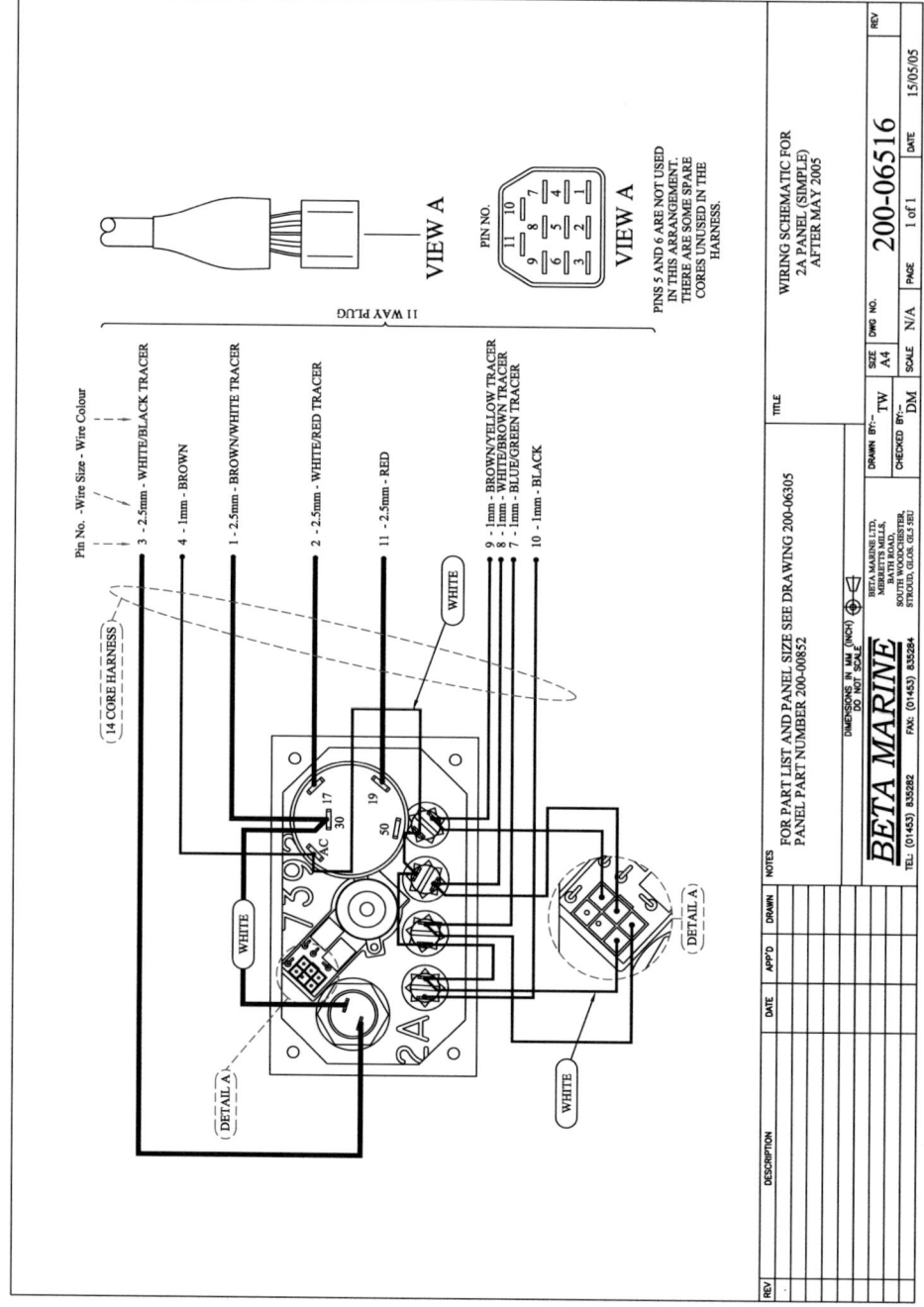

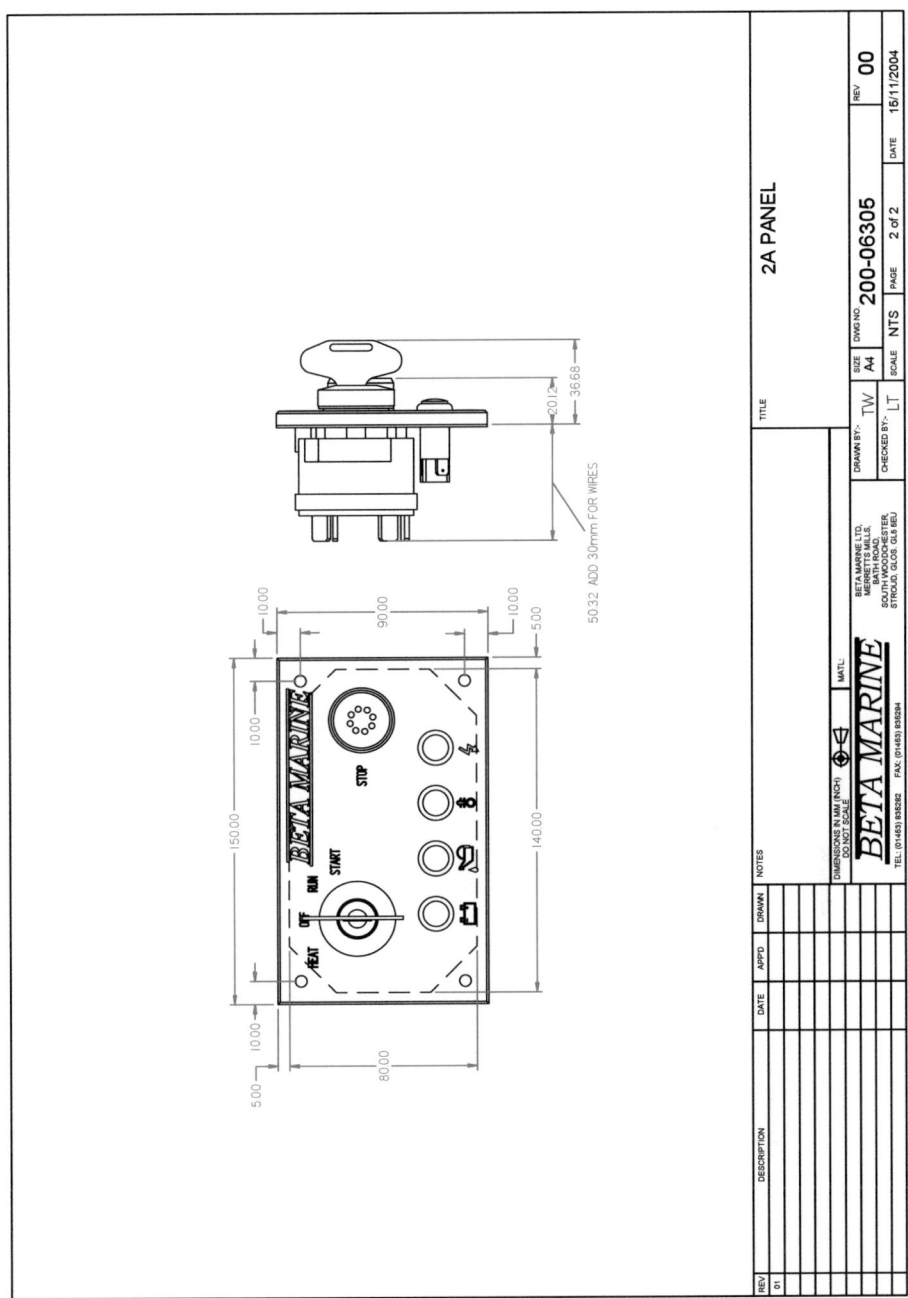

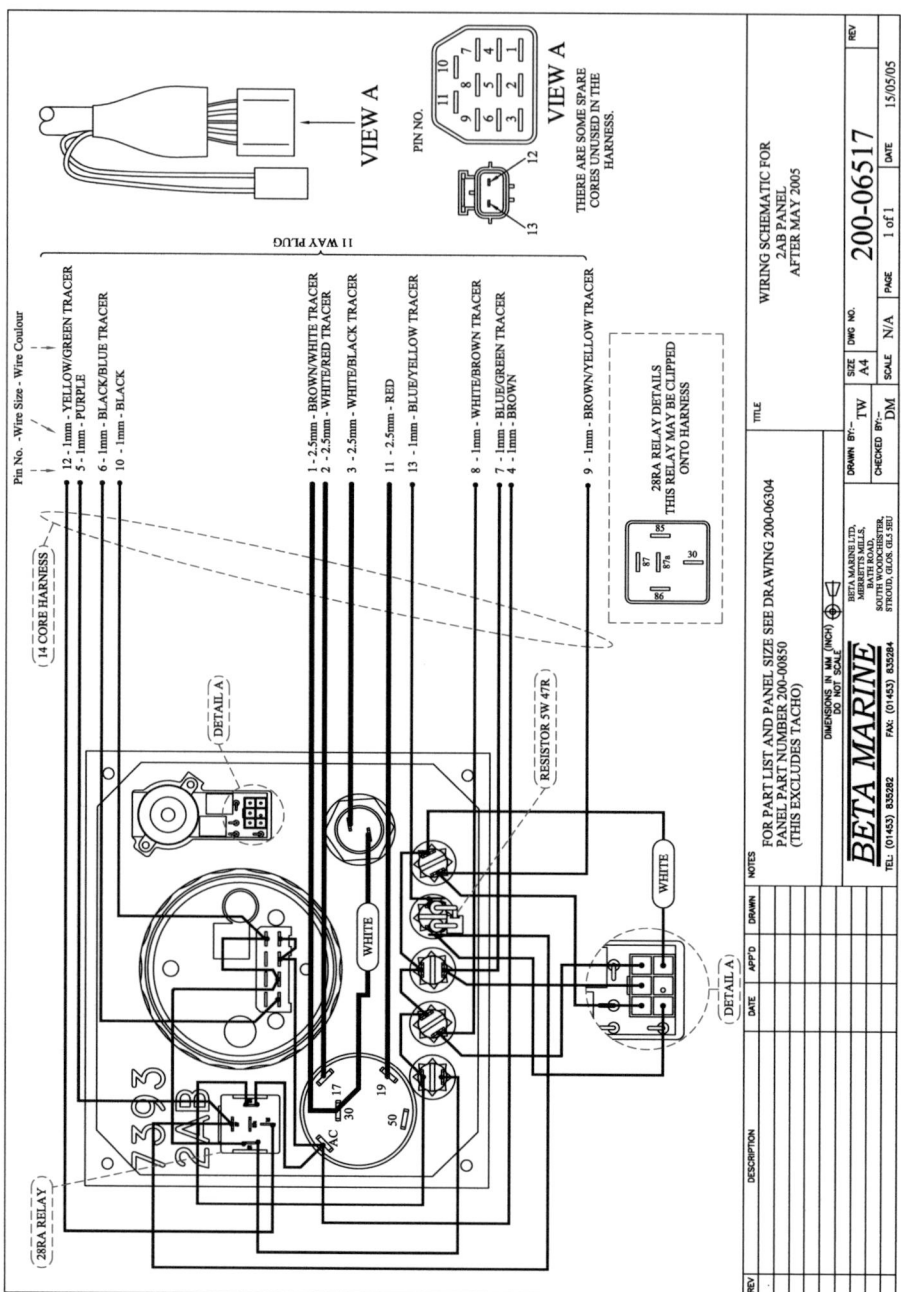

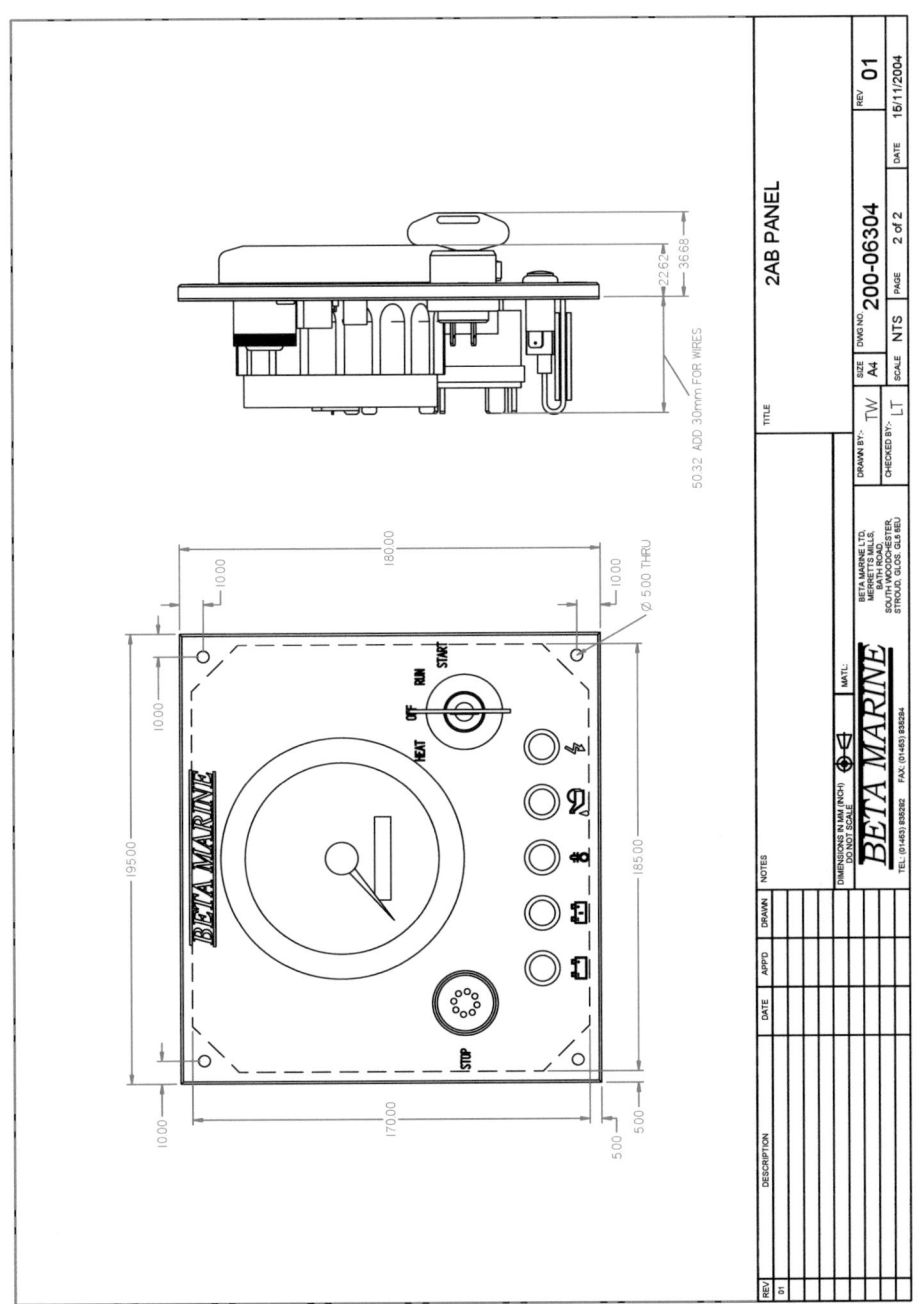

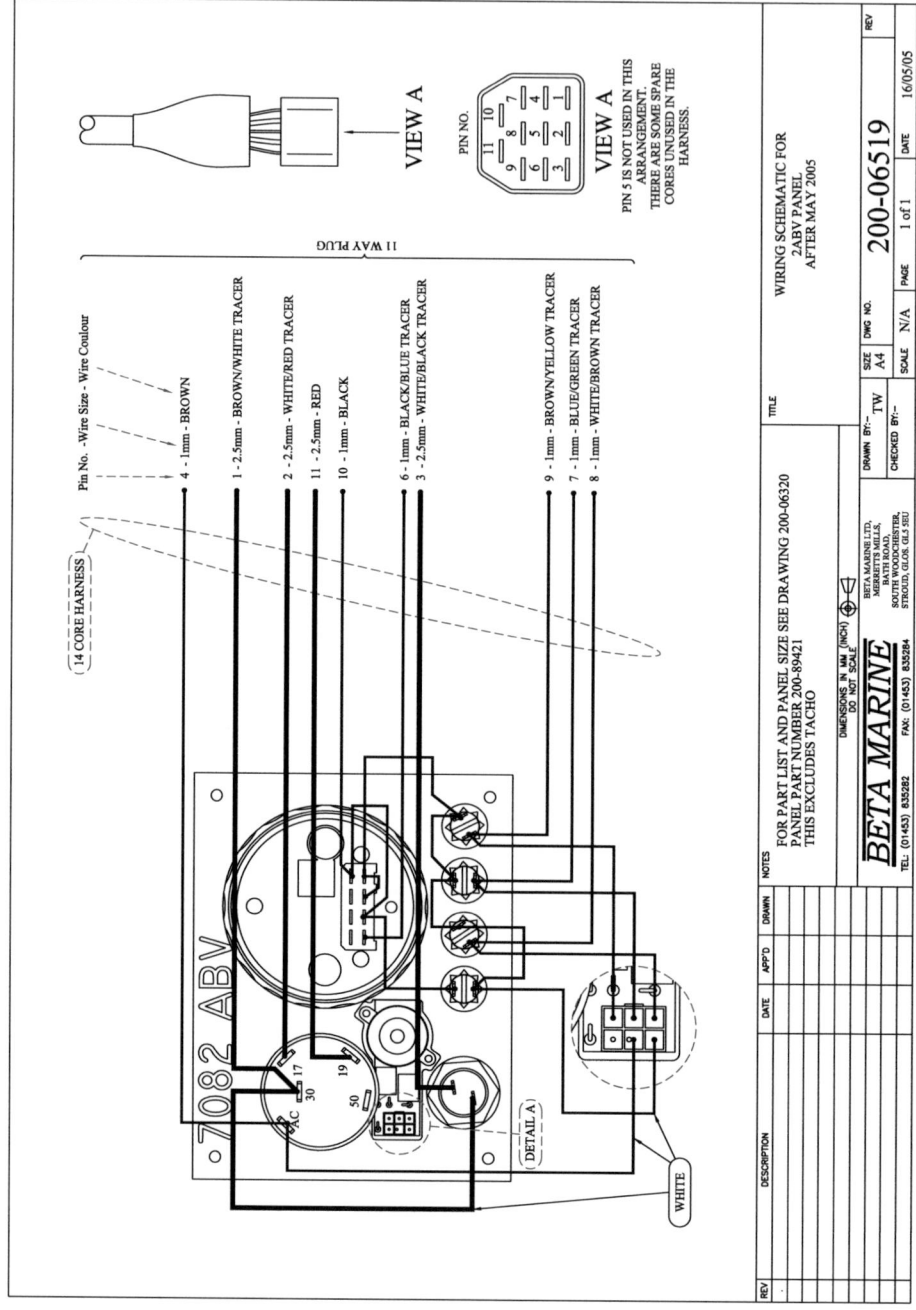

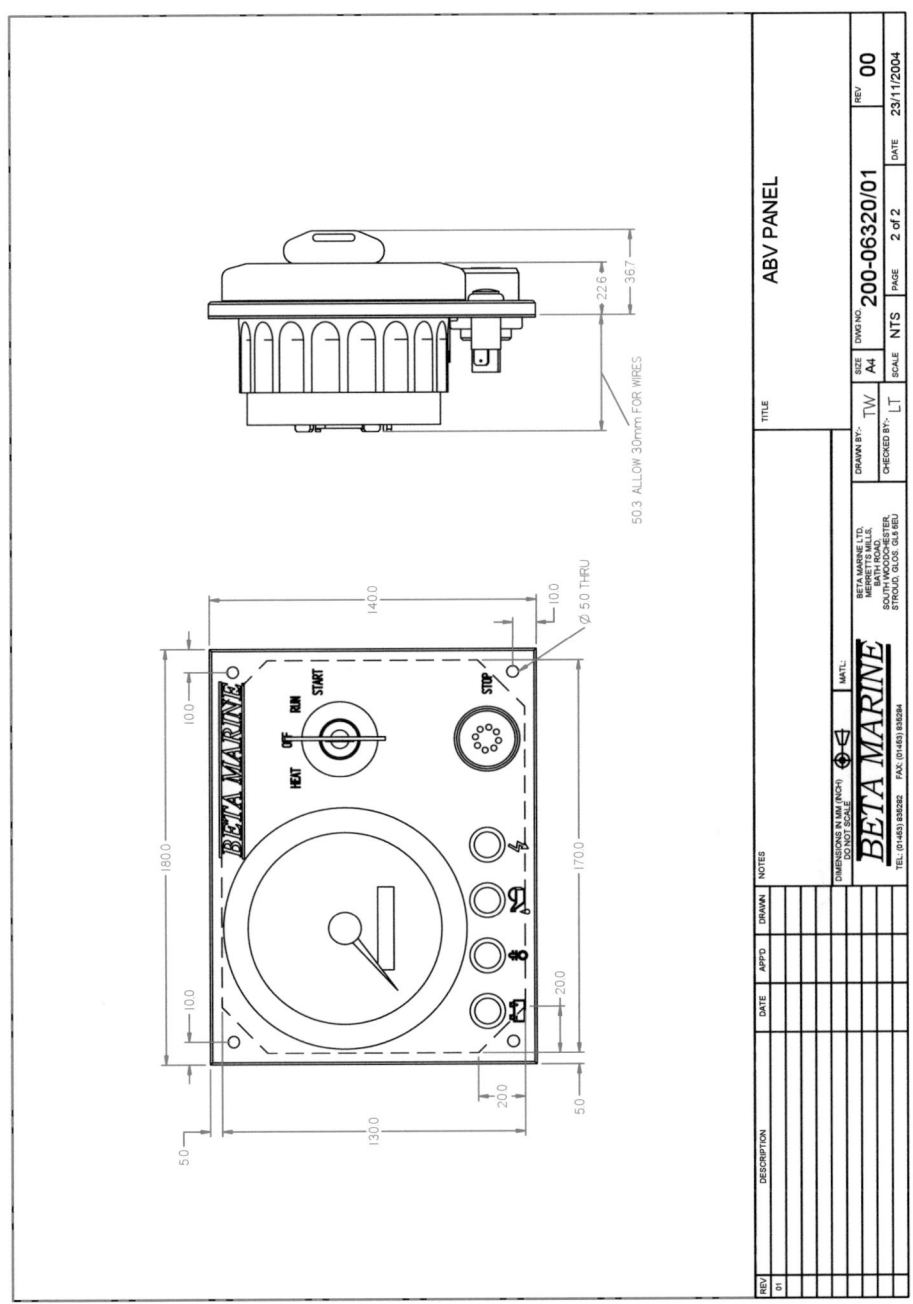

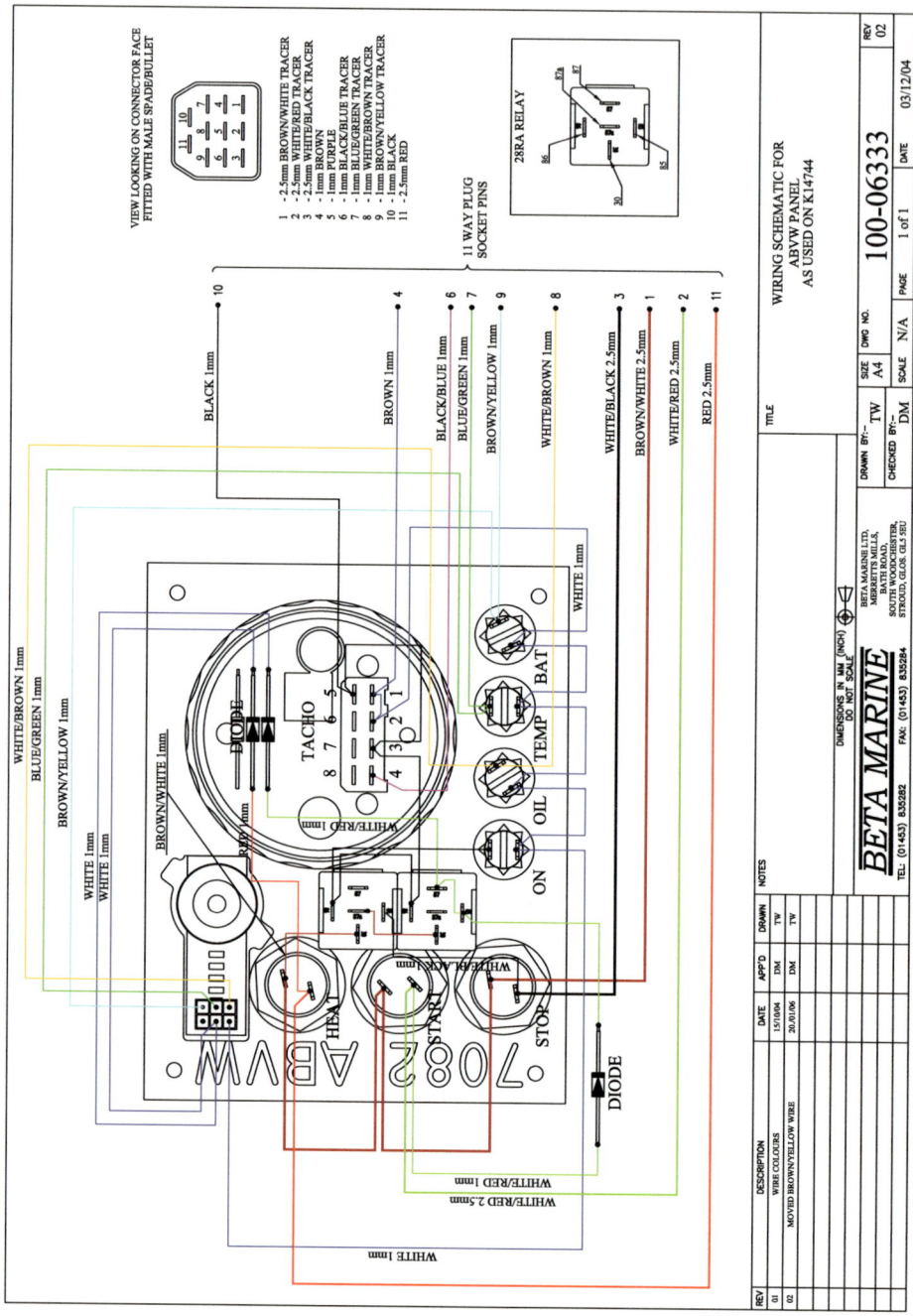

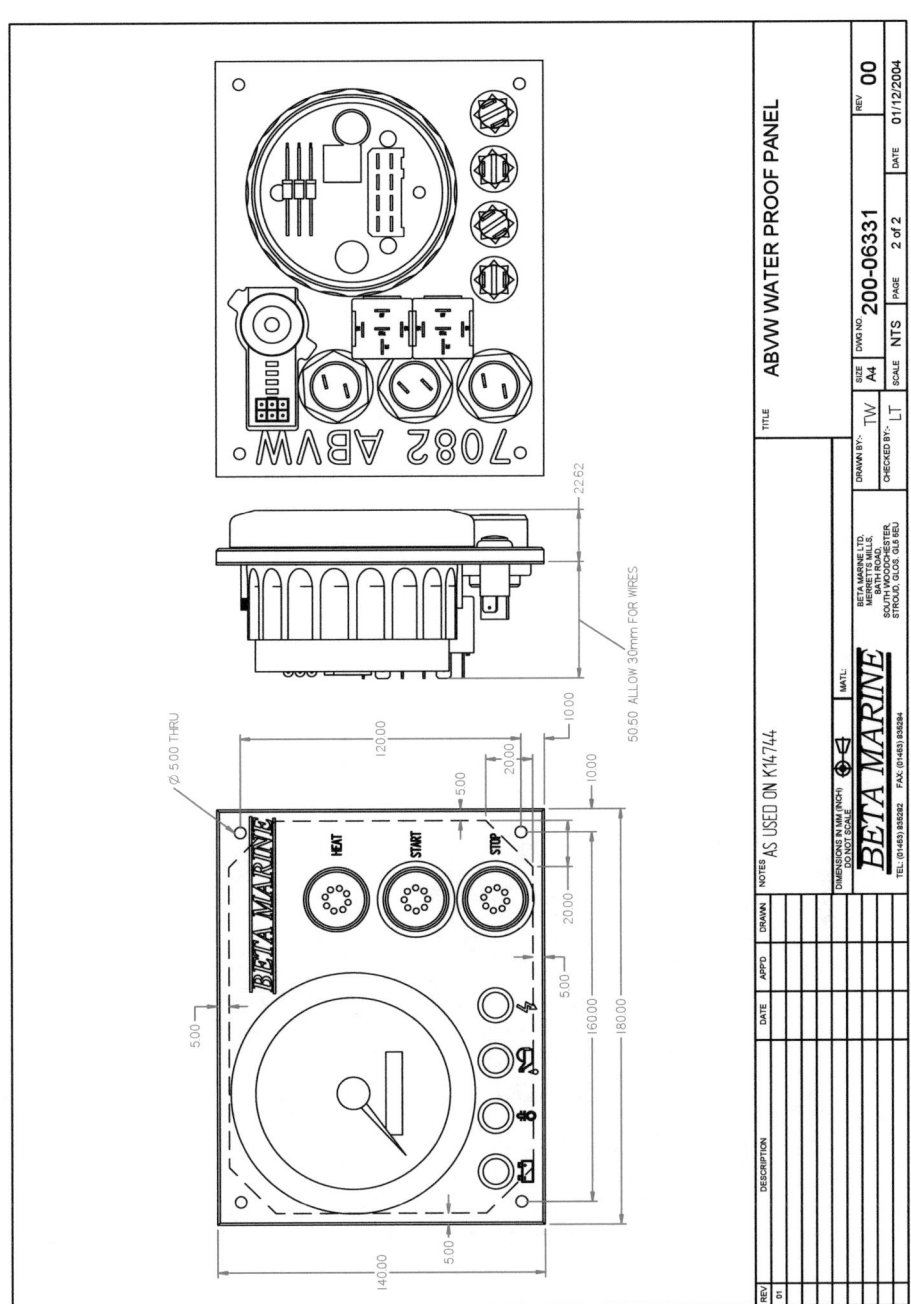

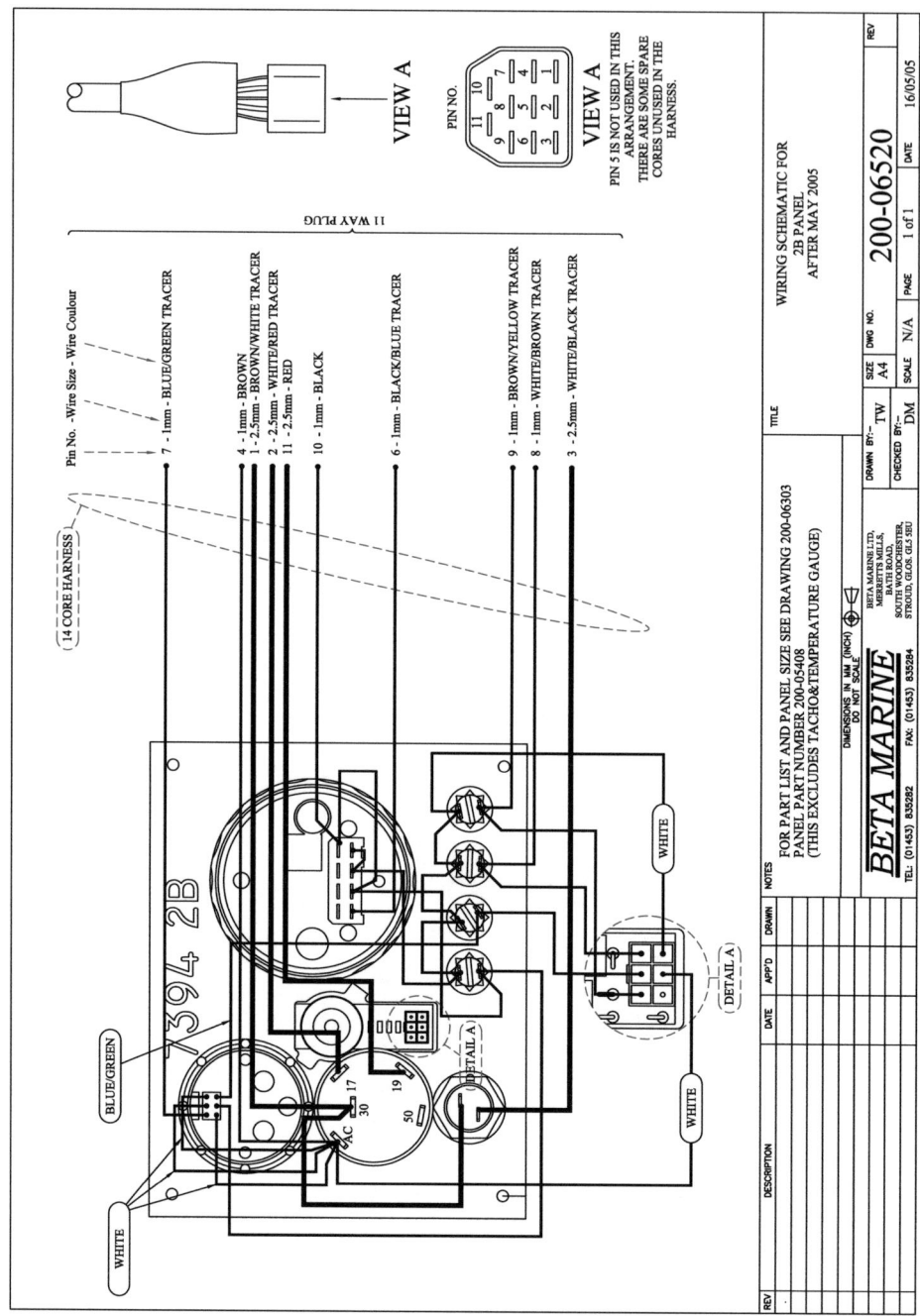

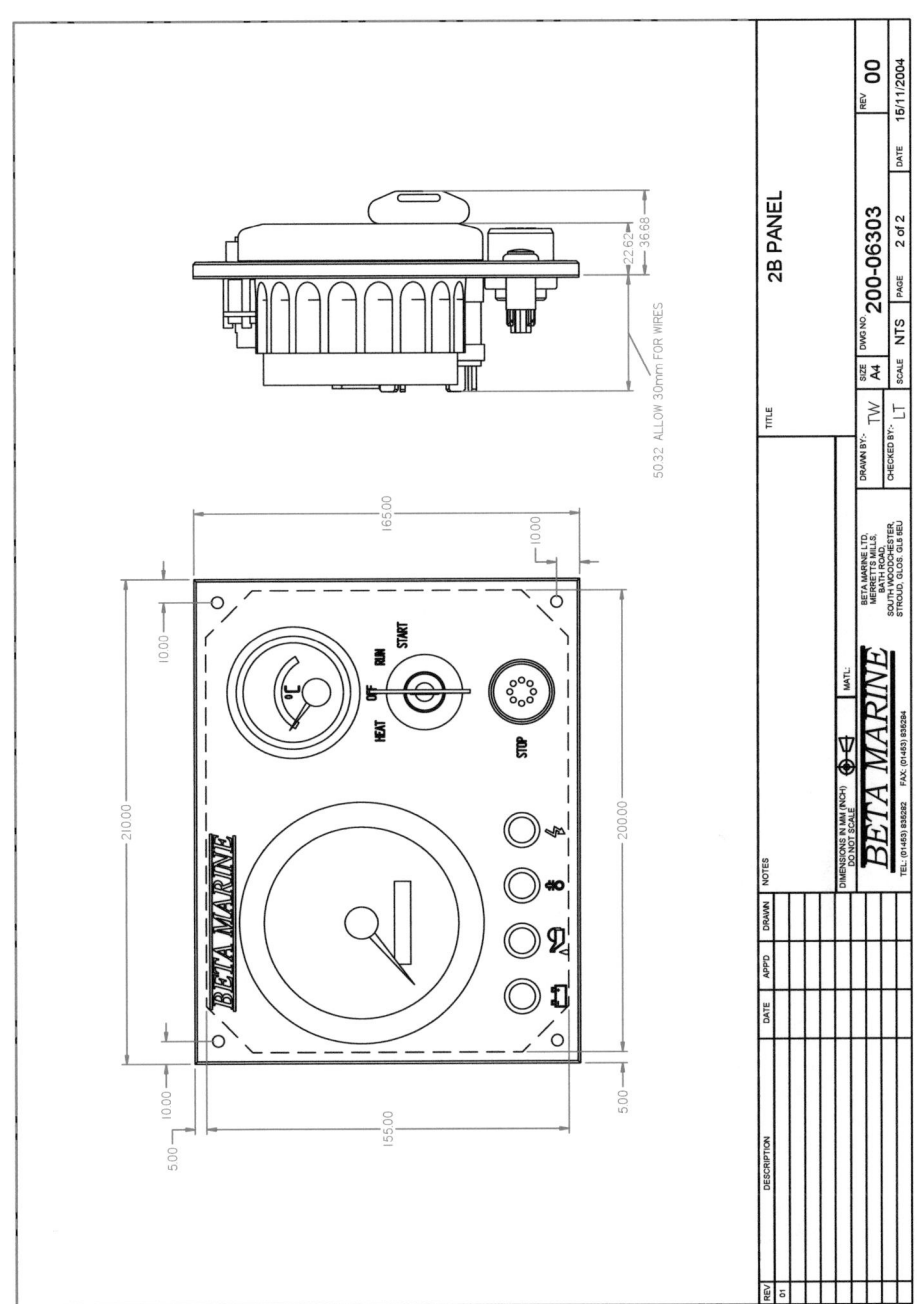

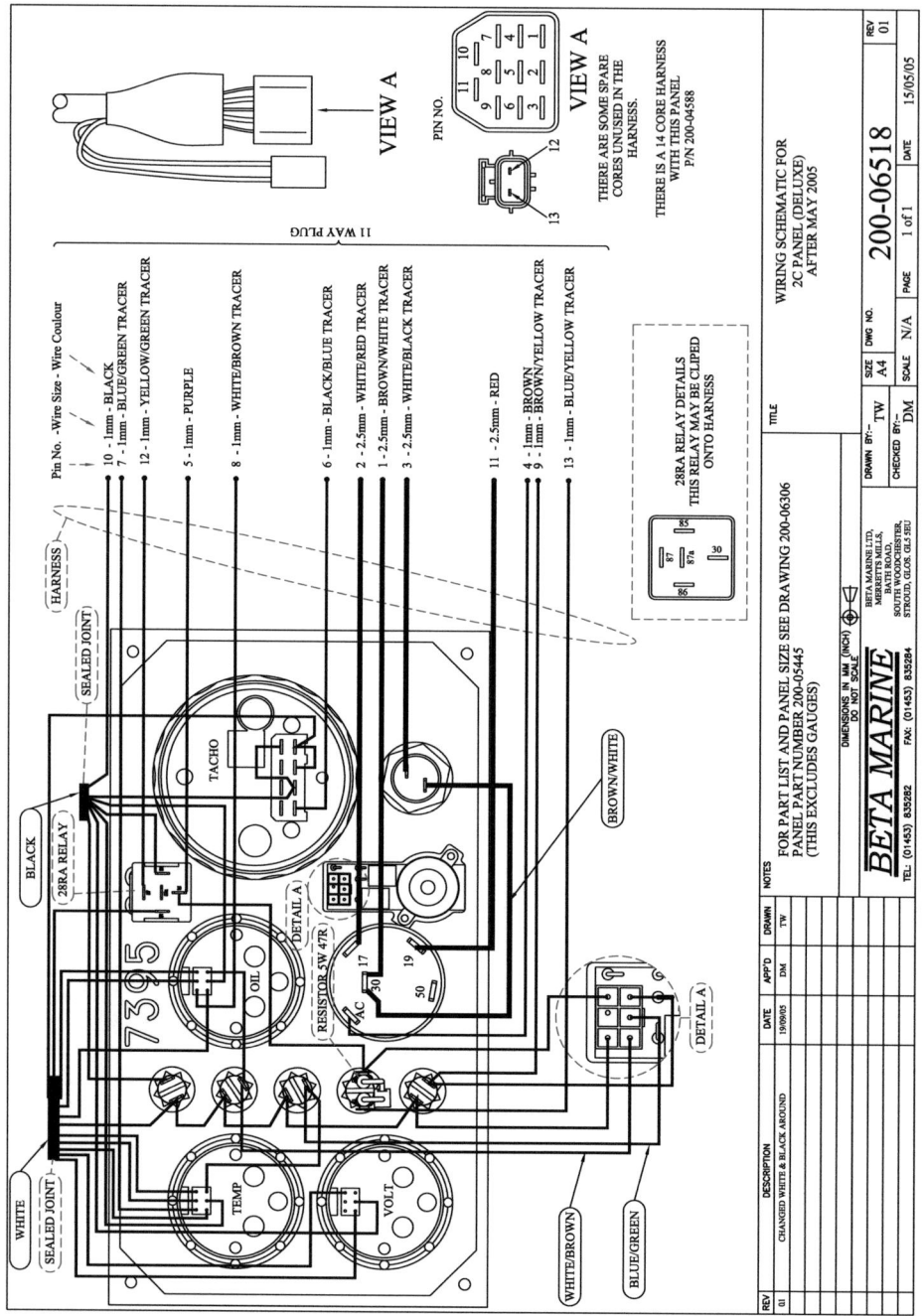

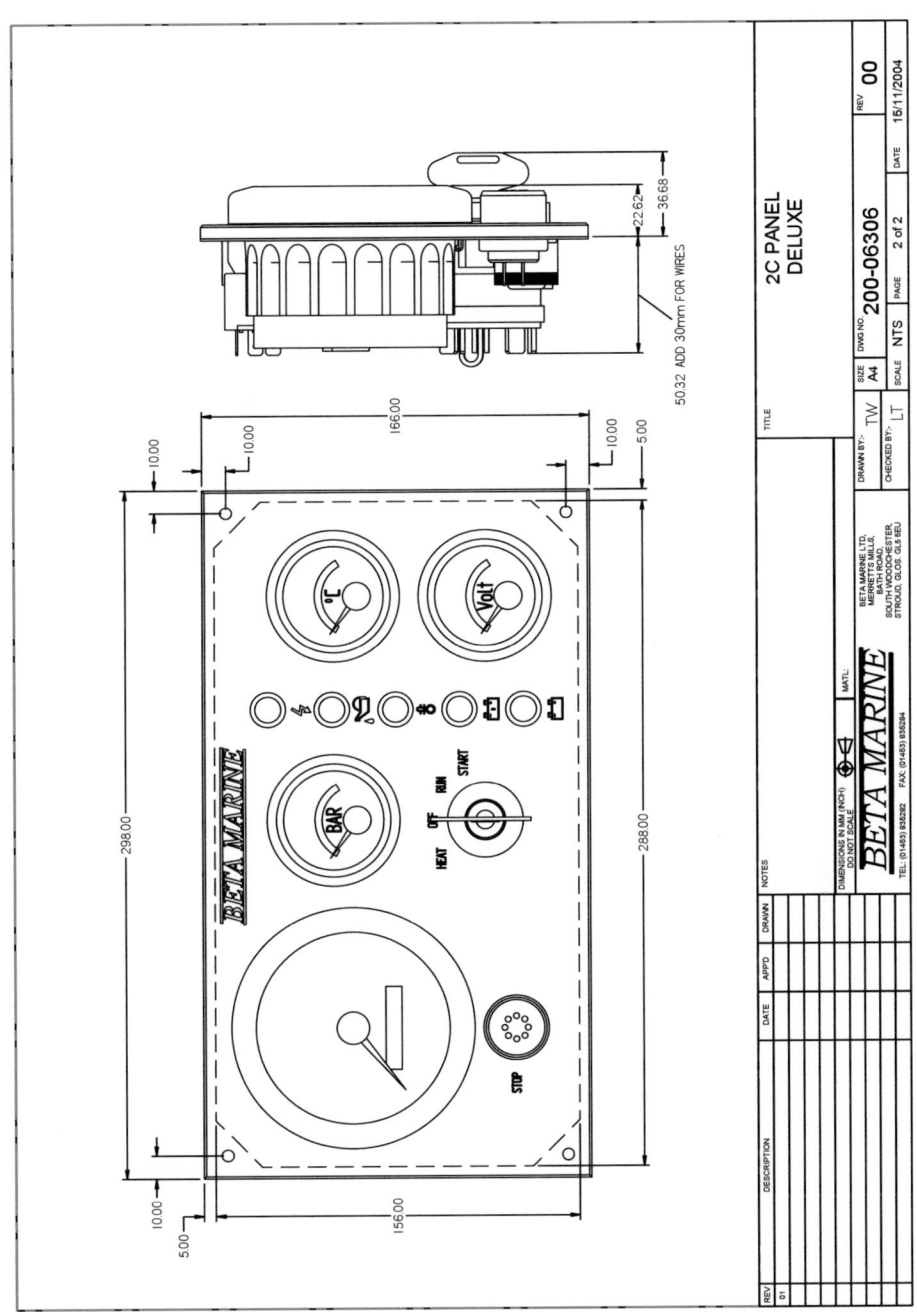

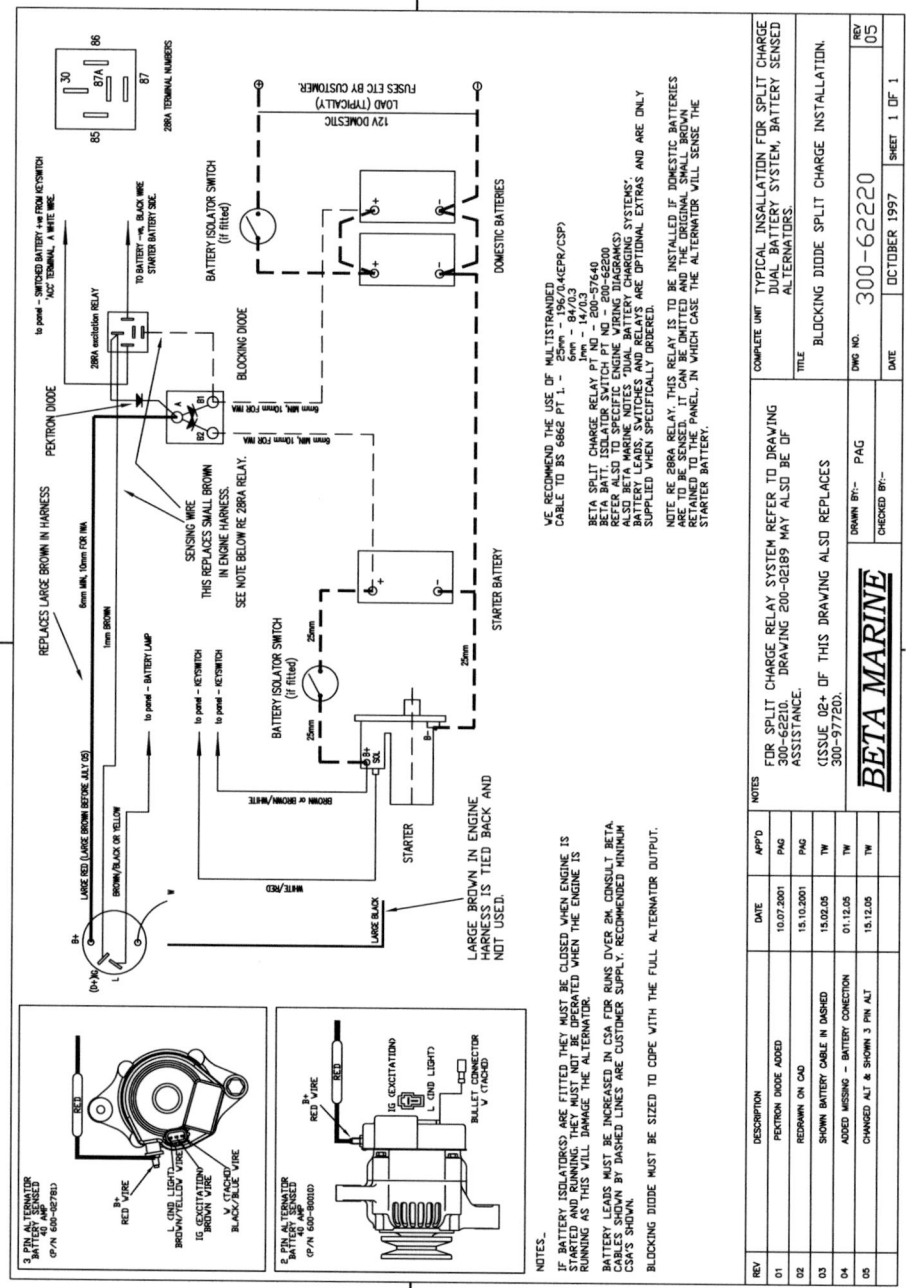

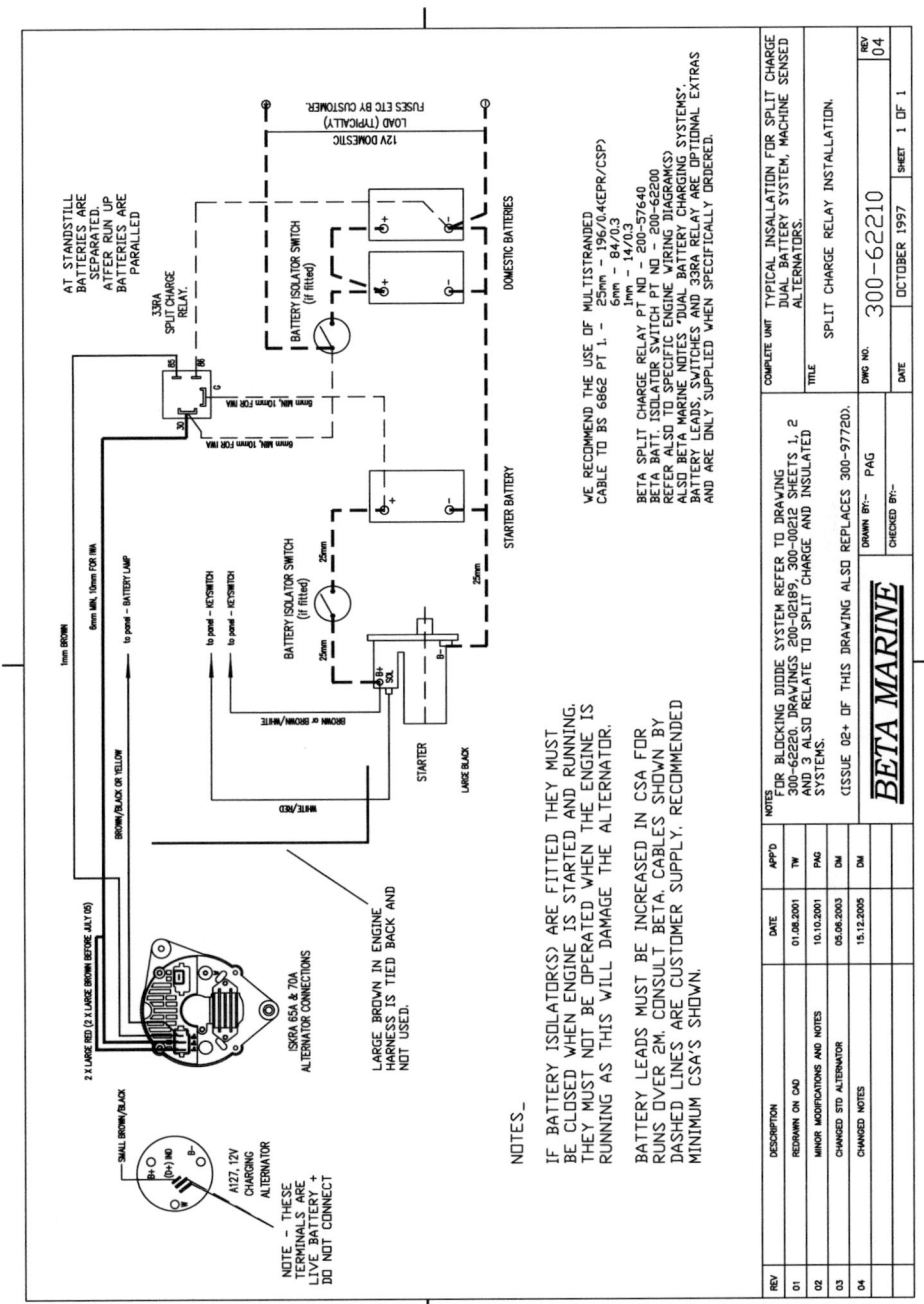

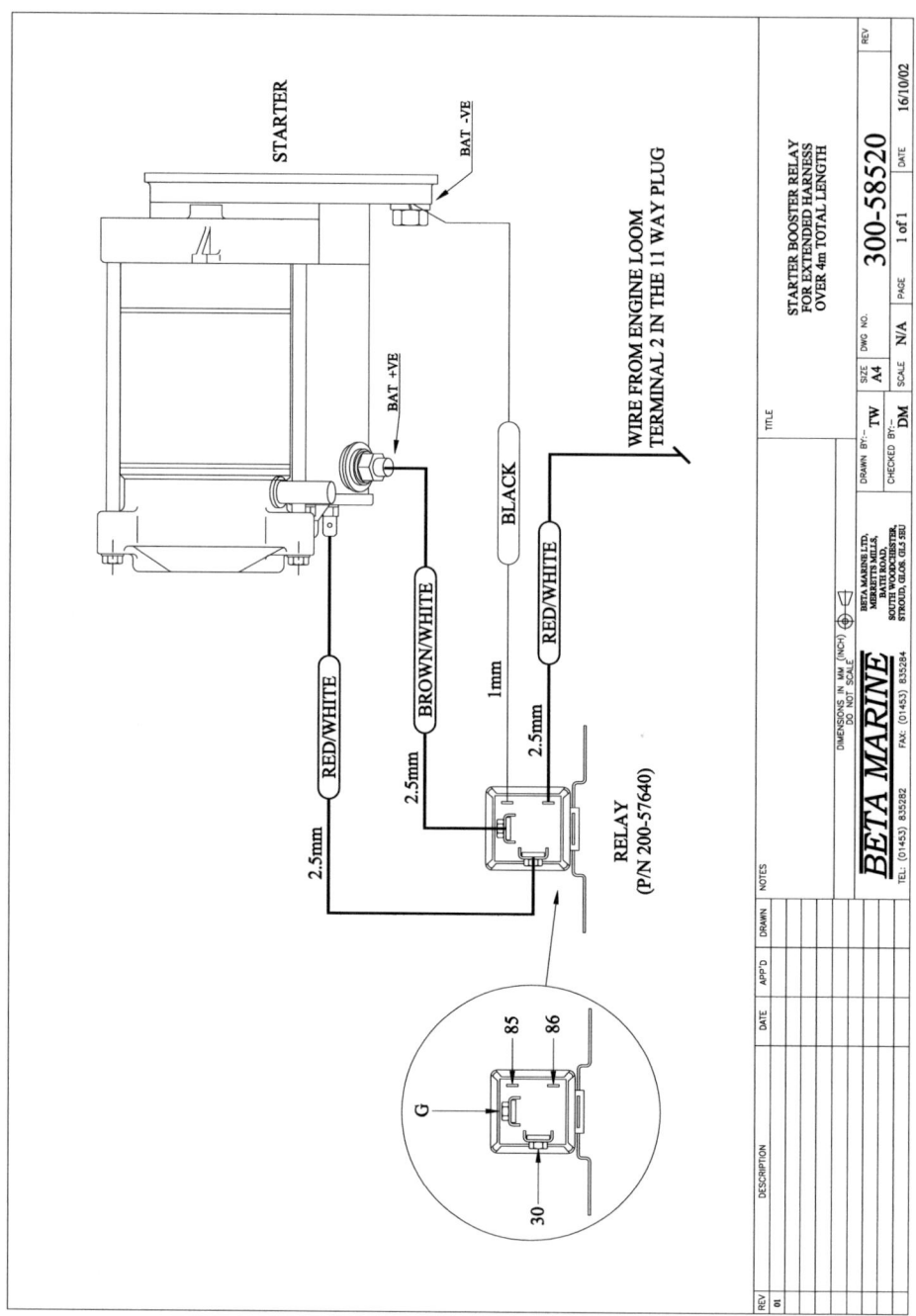

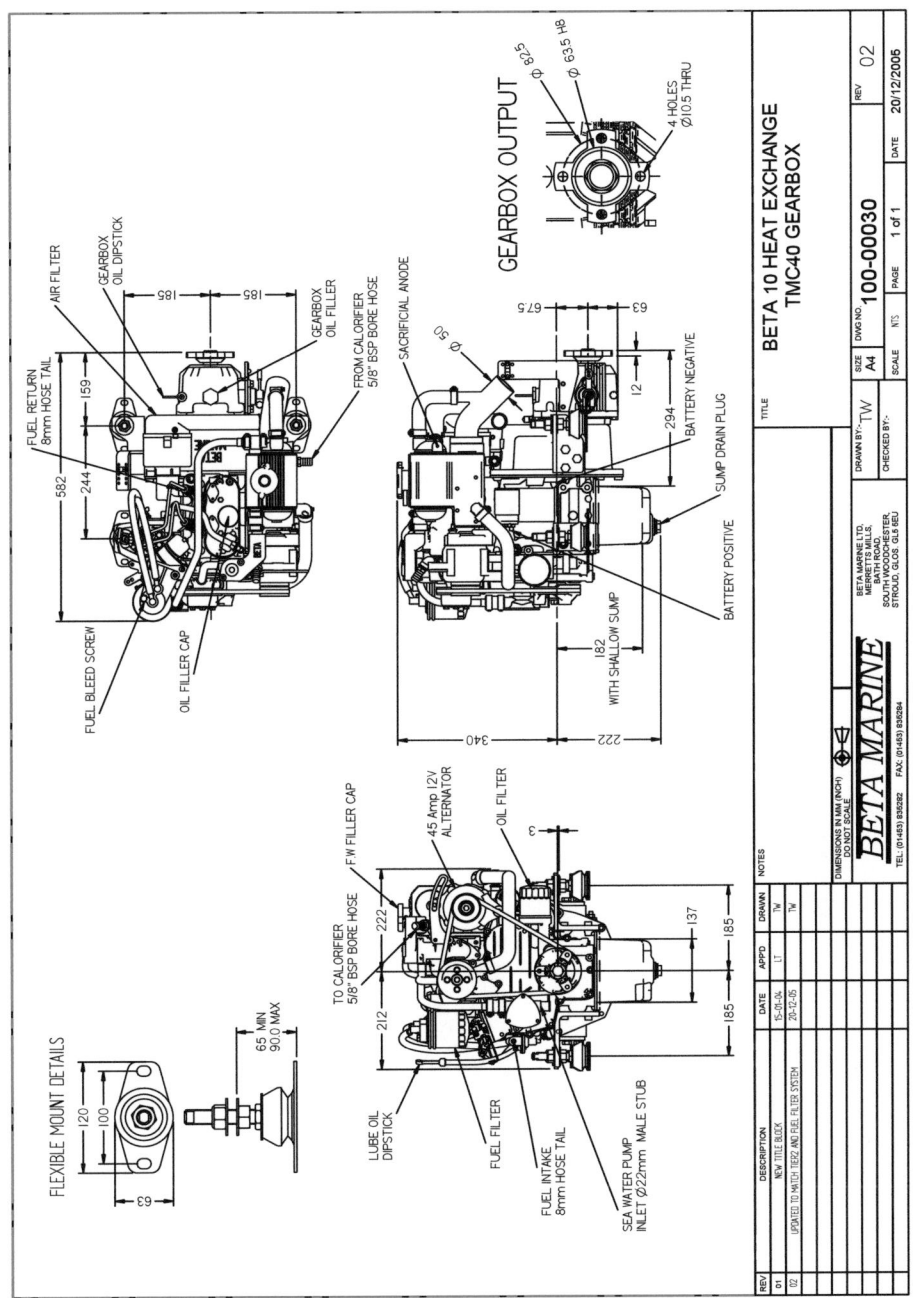

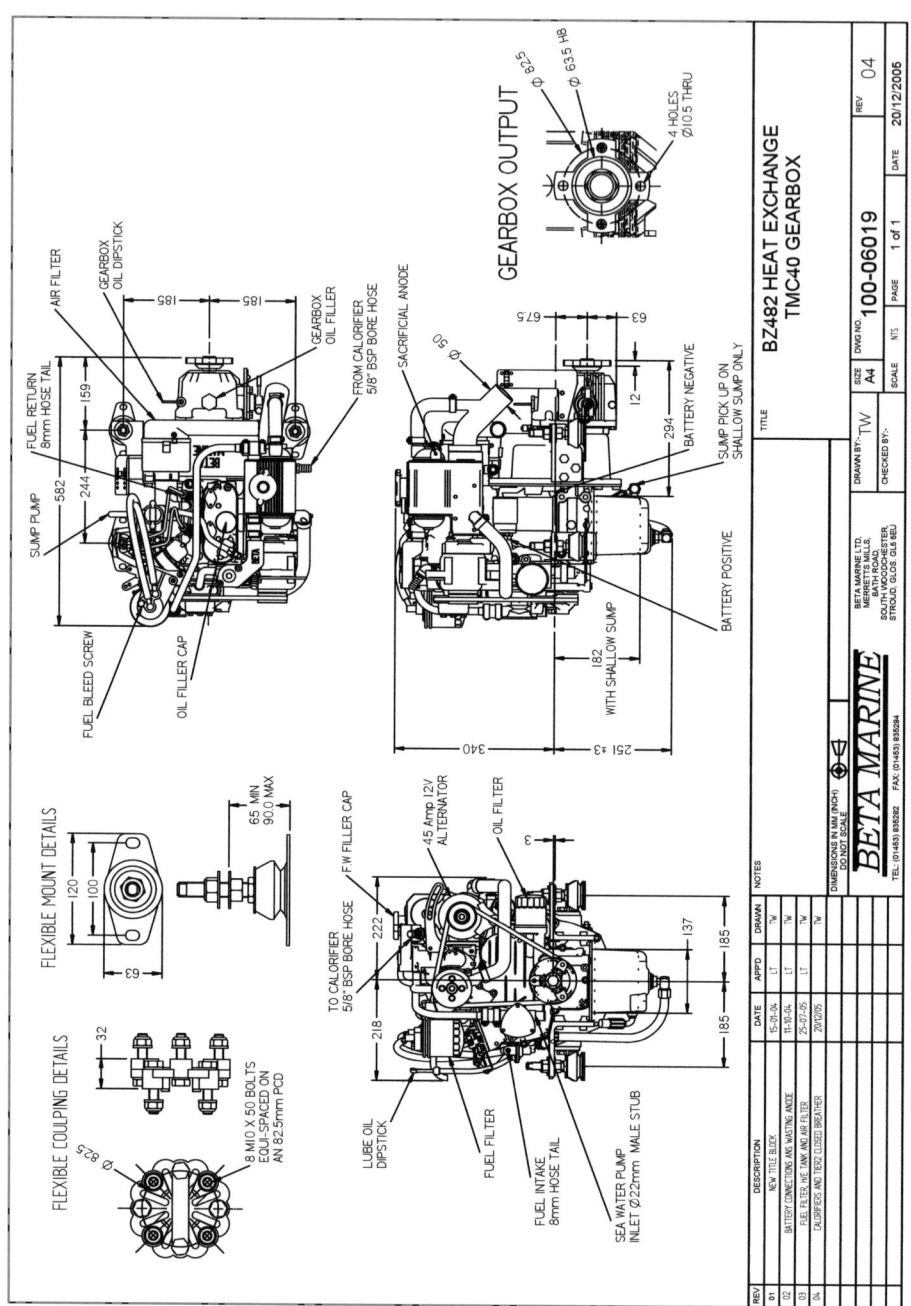

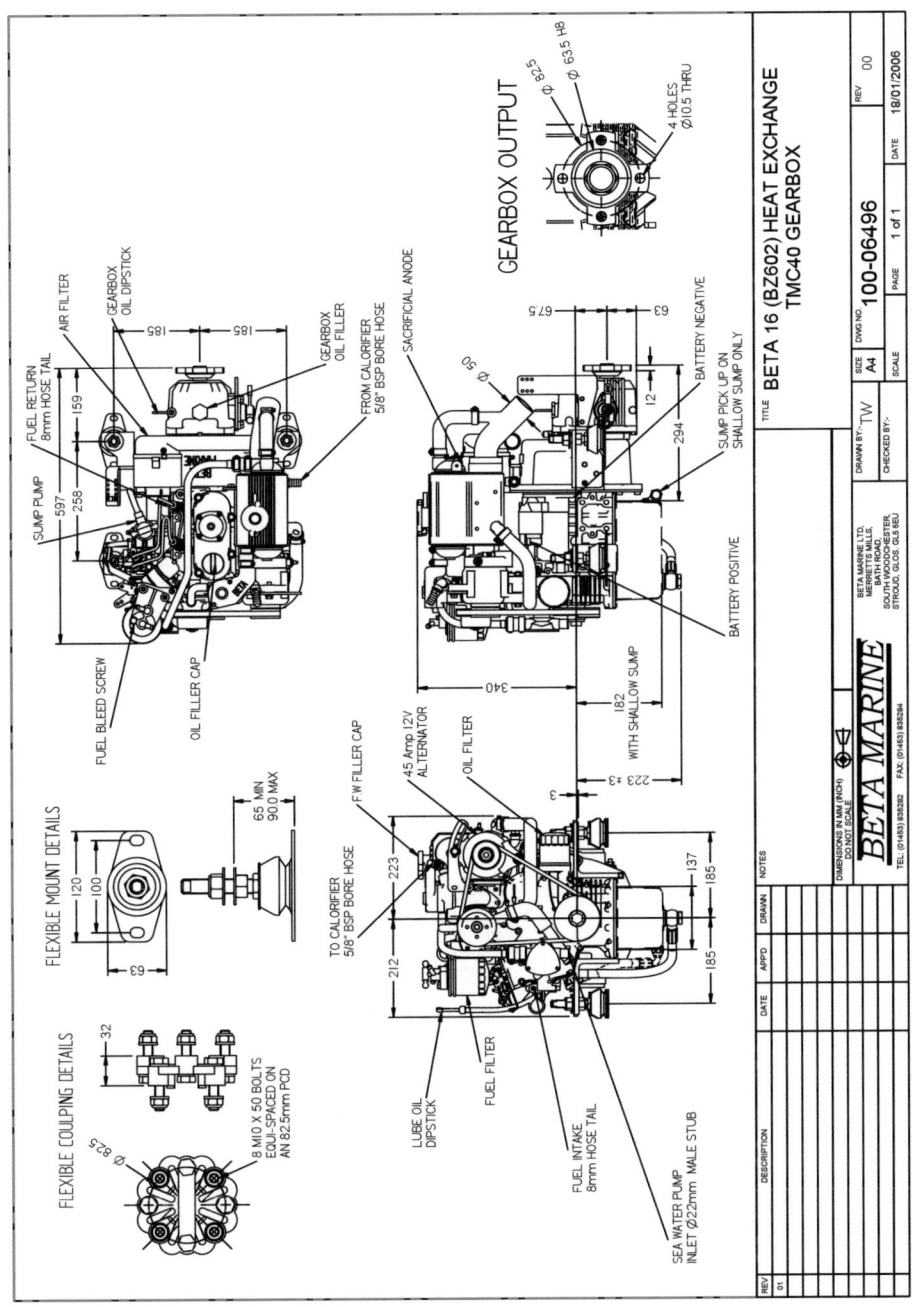

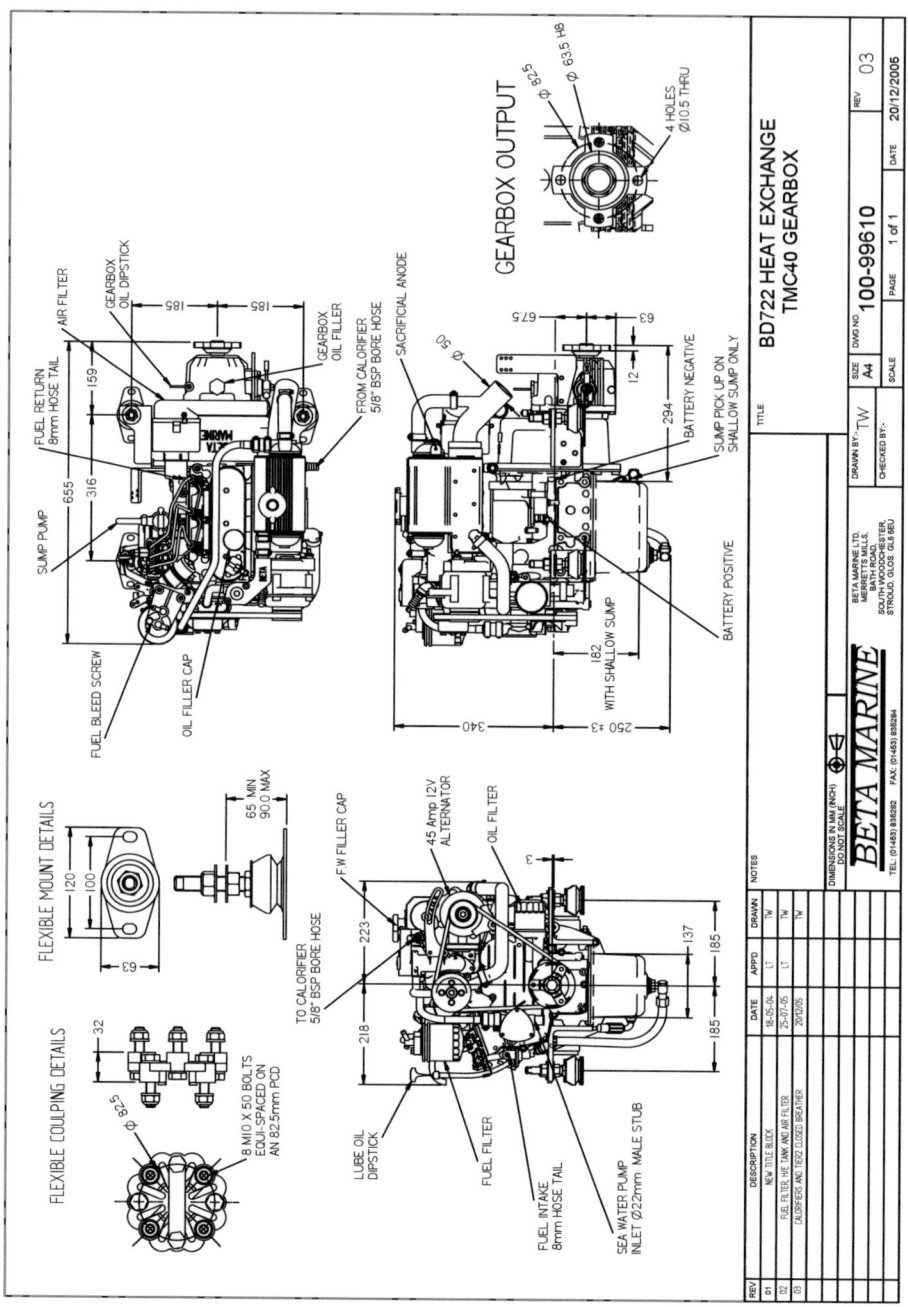

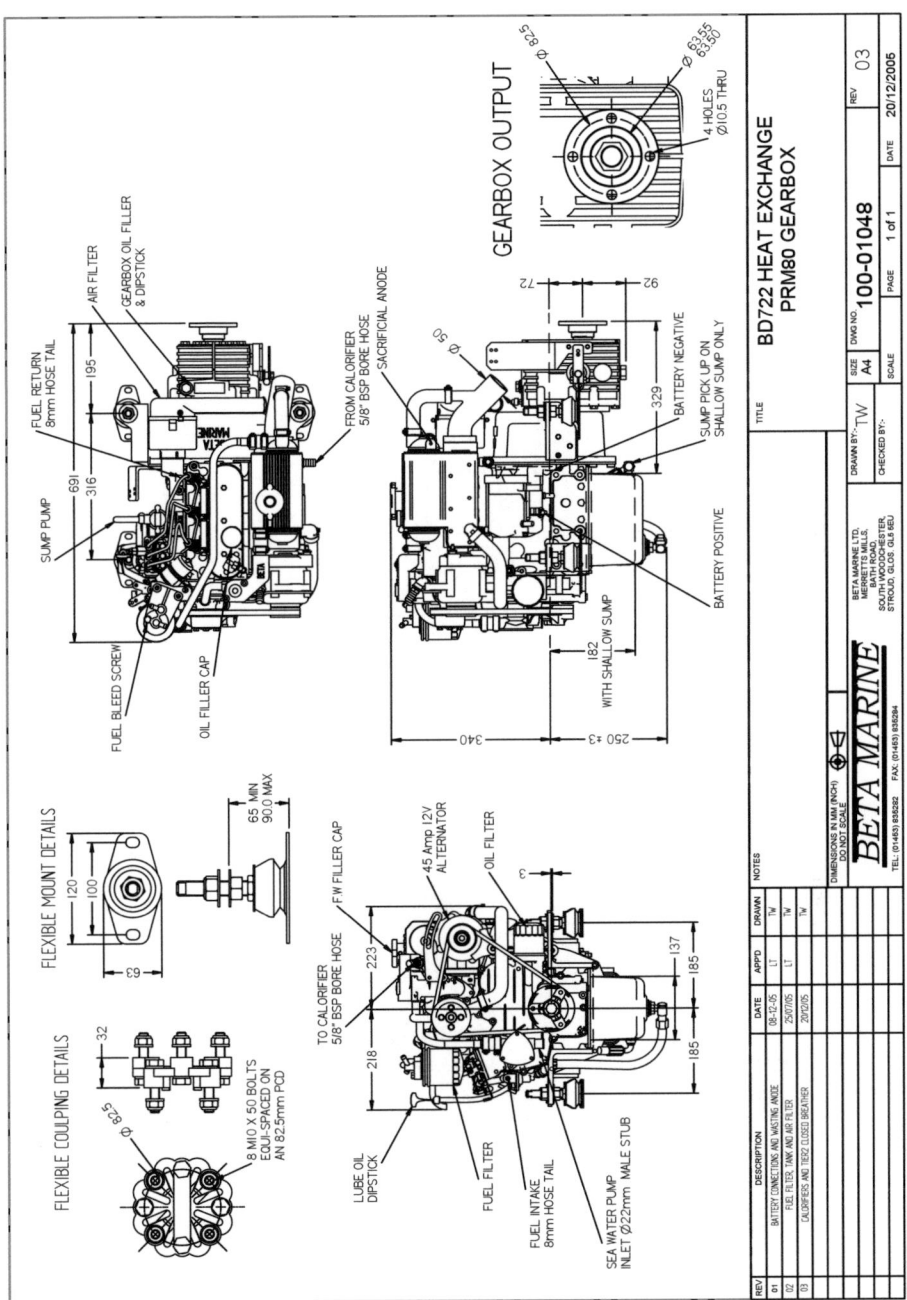

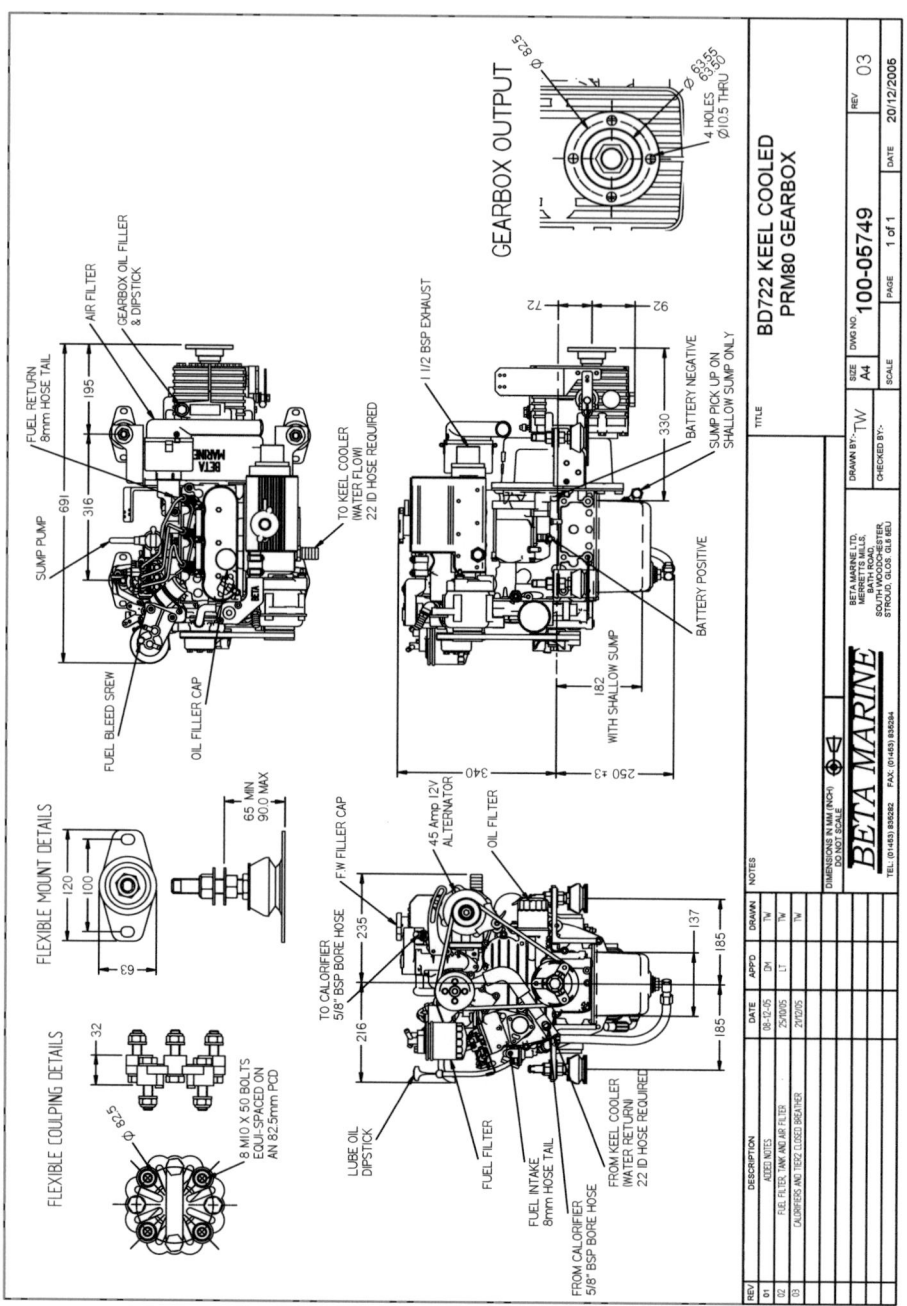

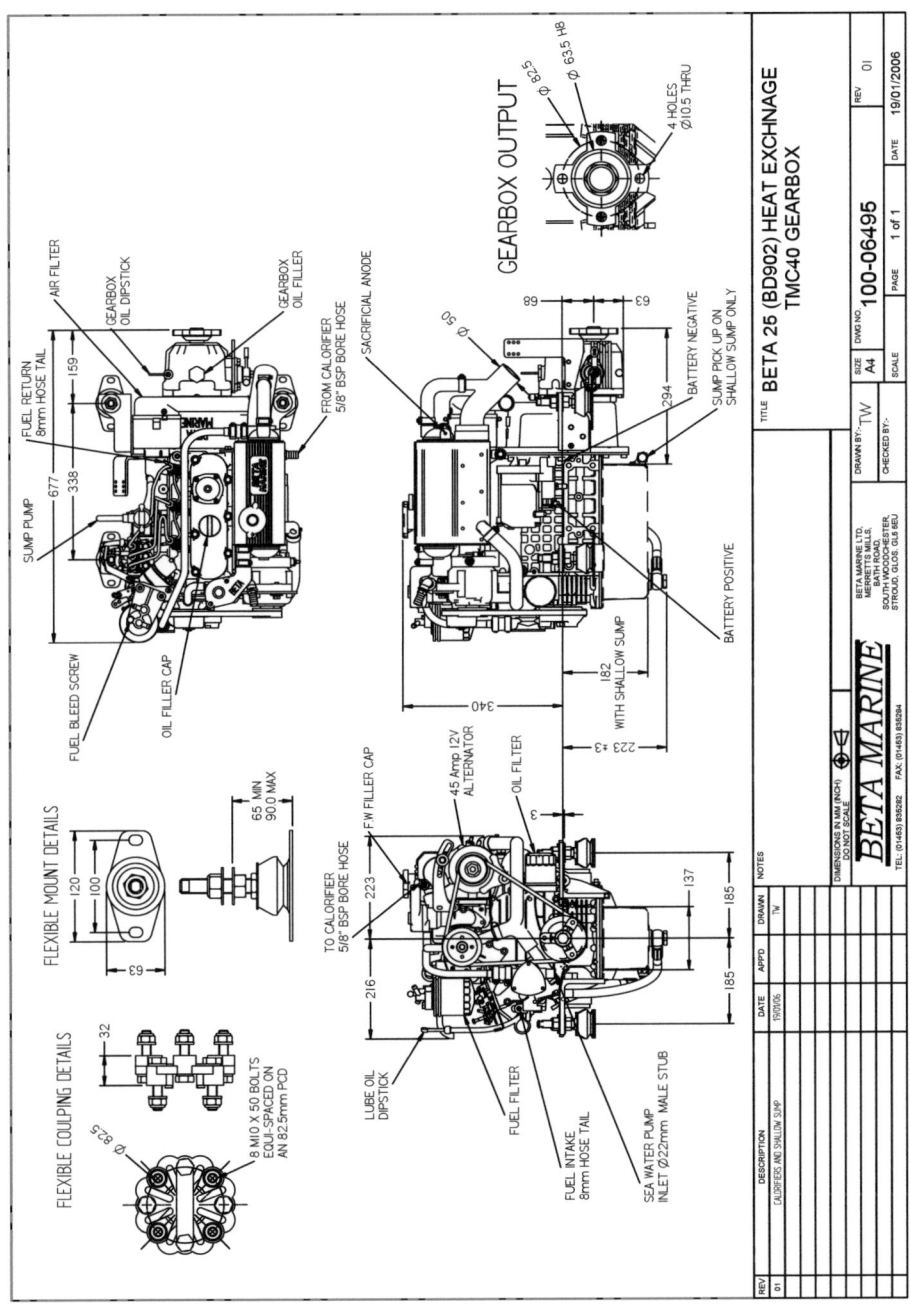

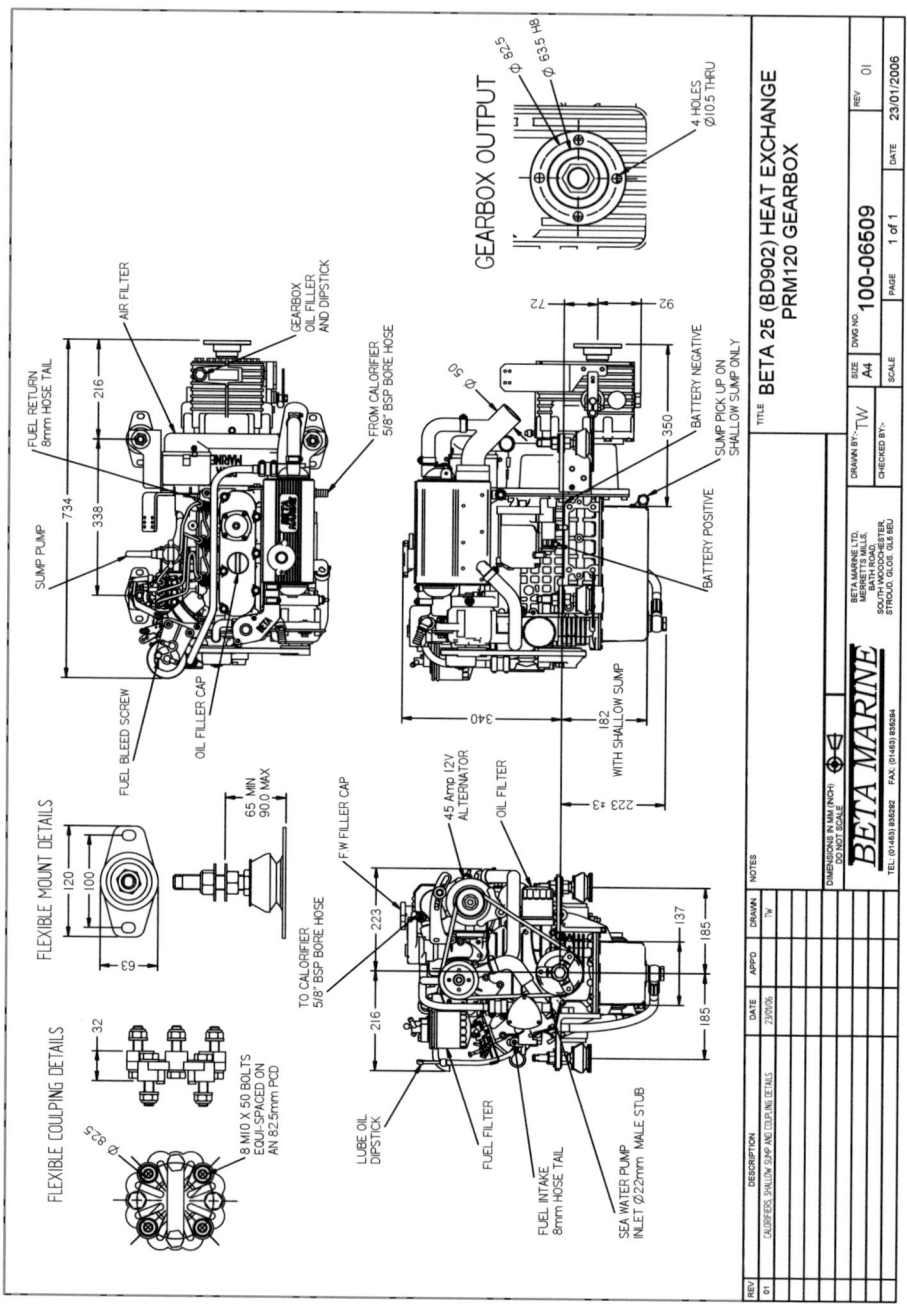

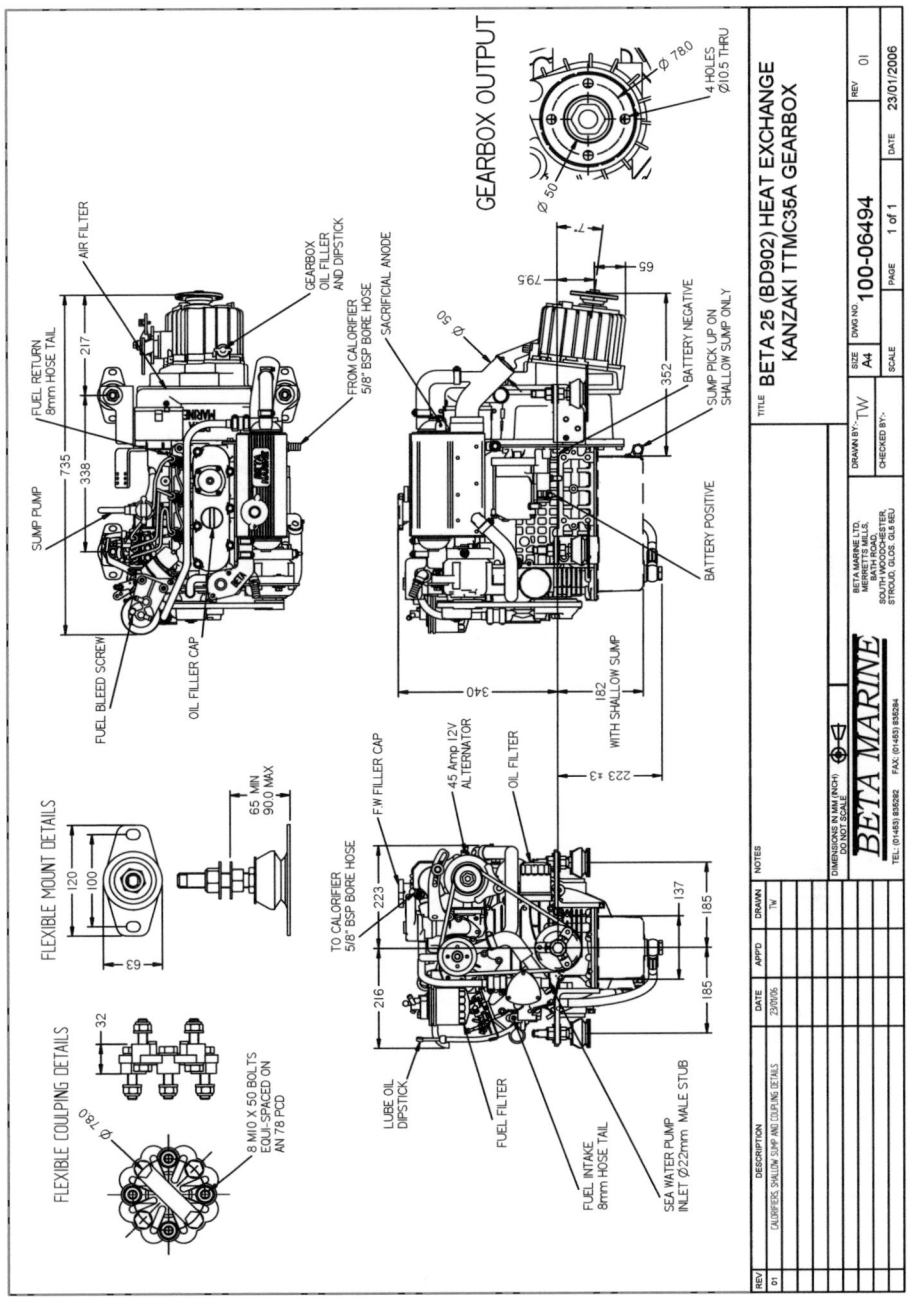

QUICK REFERENCE PARTS LISTING

Heat Exchanger & Keel Cooled Beta 10, BZ482, Beta 16, BD722, & Beta 25

In all cases please quote Beta Marine WOC "K" number and Engine Type

Description	Part Number	Qty per Engine
Alarm board	200-04655	1
Relay 12 Volt 40A (28Ra) fitted to rear of panels	200-87020	1
Stop Solenoid (energised to stop fuel)	600-81950	1
Fuse (Blade) 40 Amp	200-00959	1
Standard Engine Harness	200-98380/01	1
65 Amp Alternator Sub Loom (external fan)	200-01196	
1m Panel Extension Loom	200-04588/01	
2m Panel Extension Loom	200-04588/02	1
3m Panel Extension Loom	200-04588/03	
4m Panel Extension Loom	200-04588/04	
Water Temperature Switch (Panel A, ABV & ABVW) NOT Beta 16 or 25	200-01133	
Water Temperature Switch with single terminal Beta 16 & Beta 25)	600-62820	1
Water Temperature Sender (Panel C & B)	200-94360	
Oil Pressure Switch (Panel A, ABV, ABVW, & B)	600-62670	1
Oil Pressure Sender (Panel C)	200-94350	
Standard 50mm Water Injection Exhaust Bend	202-02458	1
5" High Rise 50mm Water Injection Exhaust Bend	202-92400/22	
Exhaust Bend Gasket	600-62620	1
Drive Plate 22-B-60 - PRM / ZF	206-91950	1
Drive Plate 22-B-4 - TMC / ZF	206-97041	
Flexible Mountings (Trelleborg RA60)	213-93440	4
Rocker Cover Gasket BZ482	600-01055	
Rocker Cover Gasket Beta 16	600-05467	1
Rocker Cover Gasket BD722	600-00607	
Rocker Cover Gasket Beta 25	600-05468	
Head Gasket Beta 10, BZ482	600-00409	
Head Gasket Beta 16	600-05469	1
Head Gasket BD722	600-01562	
Head Gasket Beta 25	600-05470	
Top Gasket Set BZ482	600-00383	
Top Gasket Set Beta 16	600-05471	1
Top Gasket Set BD722	600-00395	
Top Gasket Set Beta 25	600-05472	
Lower Gasket Set BZ482	600-01056	
Lower Gasket Set Beta 16	600-05473	1
Lower Gasket Set BD722	600-00394	
Lower Gasket Set Beta 25	600-05474	
Manuals		
Operators Maintenance Manual	221-02887	1
Kubota Workshop Manual, Beta 10 / BZ482, BD722	600-00756	1
Kubota Workshop Manual, Beta 16 & Beta 25	600-05475	
Kubota Spare Parts Manual - Beta 10 & BZ482	600-02437	
Kubota Spare Parts Manual – Beta 16	600-05476	1
Kubota Spare Parts Manual – BD722	600-02438	
Kubota Spare Parts Manual - Beta 25	600-05477	

QUICK REFERENCE PARTS LISTING

Heat Exchanger & Keel Cooled Beta 10, BZ482, Beta 16, BD722, & Beta 25

In all cases please quote Beta Marine WOC "K" number and Engine Type

Description	Part Number	Qty per Engine
Wasting **Zinc Anode**	209-61840	1
Heat Exchanger **"O" Ring**	209-80110	2
Pressure Cap 95kPa	209-80130	1
Thermostat	600-59290	1
Thermostat (Beta 16 & 25 only)	600-72450	
Thermostat **Gasket**	600-62590	1
Thermostat **Gasket** (Beta 16 & 25 only)	600-80490	
Fuel Filter	211-60210	1
Air Filter **Element**	211-62950	1
Lubricating **Oil Filter**	211-63760	1
Sump Pump	201-80061	1
Sump Pump **Clamp**	212-00793	2
Dip Stick (only) - Extended	600-96280	1
Sea Water Pump Johnson (6 Screw)	207-61500/01	
Sea Water Pump **Impeller Kit** Johnson 6 Screw (includes gasket etc.)	207-05355	1
Sea Water Pump **Cover plate** Johnson 6 Screw	207-05478	1
Sea Water Pump cover plate **Bolt** Johnson 6 Screw	207-05479	6
Fuel Lift Pump	600-65470	1
Fuel Lift Pump – Beta 16 & 25	AK/MINI/9&6/F0I	
Fuel Lift Pump **Gasket**	600-00065	1
Belt – Standard "Vee" – 40 Amp	600-63080	Correctly Select a Belt
Belt – PolyVee 40 Amp 4PK900 (NOT Beta 25)	214-04360	
Belt – PolyVee 40 Amp 4PK913 Beta 25	214-05074	
Belt – 65 Amp Alternator BZ482/BD722 - 4PK950 – External fan	214-03235	
Belt – 65 Amp Alternator Beta 16 - 4PK900 – Internal fan	212-04360	
Belt – 65 Amp Alternator Beta 25 4PK913 Internal fan	214-05074	
Alternator 40 Amp	600-80010	1
Alternator 55 Amp - (A127)	200-69190	
Alternator 65 Amp – External Fan	200-01155	
Alternator 65 Amp – Internal Fan	200-04989	
Panel A - standard	AK/2AS/KS01	1
Panel ABV with tachometer	AK/2ABV/KS01	
Panel ABVW with tachometer	AK/2ABVW/KS01	
Panel B – with tachometer and gauge	AK/2BT/KS01	
Panel C – with tachometer and three gauges	AK/2CD/KS01	
Control Panel standard **Key**	600-00058	1
Control Panel **Key Switch**	600-00057	1
Control Panel **Stop Button** (and heat & start on ABVW)	200-00072	1
Tachometer 0-4000rpm with digital hour counter	200-02373	1
Water temperature switch **Gauge** (B & C panels)	200-96200	1
Oil pressure switch **Gauge** (C panels only)	200-96190	1
Voltmeter (C panels only)	200-96210	1
Green power on **indicator lamp** & retaining clip	200-04656	1
Red warning **indicator lamp** & retaining clip	200-04657	3 or 4